AIM
HIGH

AIM HIGH

HOW TO STYLE YOUR LIFE AND ACHIEVE YOUR GOALS

SYDNEY SADICK

FOREWORD BY FERN MALLIS

Skyhorse Publishing

Skyhorse Publishing books may be purchased in bulk at special discounts for sales promotion, corporate gifts, fund-raising, or educational purposes. Special editions can also be created to specifications. For details, contact the Special Sales Department, Skyhorse Publishing, 307 West 36th Street, 11th Floor, New York, NY 10018 or info@skyhorsepublishing.com.

Skyhorse® and Skyhorse Publishing® are registered trademarks of Skyhorse Publishing, Inc.®, a Delaware corporation.

Visit our website at www.skyhorsepublishing.com.

10 9 8 7 6 5 4 3 2 1

Library of Congress Cataloging-in-Publication Data is available on file.

Cover design by Brian Peterson
Cover photo credit: Steve Erle Photography

Print ISBN: 978-1-5107-5904-6
Ebook ISBN: 978-1-5107-5905-3

Printed in the United States of America

To all the fashion lovers . . .

CONTENTS

FOREWORD

By Fern Mallis
New York Fashion Week Creator

"A Force of Nature" is a phrase that is often loosely thrown around, but if anyone needs a definition of this expression . . . meet Sydney Sadick. She knows how to *Aim High* and leave the Energizer Bunny in the dust . . .

Sydney had an uncanny working knowledge of the fashion industry—the designers, events, and celebrations—before she ever stepped foot inside the IMG offices where I worked. This is where the *Daily Front Row* was birthed as a publication to be given out during New York Fashion Week in the tents at Bryant Park. That's when I first met Sydney and I hadn't realized she had already been working for the publication since her senior year in high school as an intern after she brazenly wrote to them at sixteen saying she wanted a column in the *Daily*. She then freelanced all through her college years while studying journalism in the School of Media and Public Affairs at George Washington University. She definitely earned that degree and has done it proud.

During college she came into the city whenever she could to attend and report on New York Fashion Week, special industry events, and parties, including covering the "red carpet" at the famous Met Gala. She was not shy as she introduced herself to everyone, put a recorder in their face, and asked questions. She got the soundbites and the stories, and always included my opinion in her coverage as well. She became a fixture and integral part of the press corps that followed everything and anything happening in the fashion universe.

Sydney is young, energetic, tireless, and ambitious . . . in the very best sense of that often-maligned word. She clearly always knew what she wanted to do, and knew what she loved: fashion, clothes, beauty, makeup, style, fitness and design. Sydney understood instinctively—or maybe it is in her DNA—how clothes communicate self-confidence. She knew what she wanted to wear when she was in pre-school. She followed her passion from her earliest years observing her great-grandmother Helen and grandmother Hannah. Now she proudly wears pieces that she shopped in Hannah's closet such as timeless Chanel jackets and quilted gold chain handbags, and in her inimitable style combines them with her H&M or Zara leggings and tops.

Sydney also has one of the most exceptional relationships with her mother Amy, who nurtured and encouraged her and supports her at every step of her exploding career as a fashion expert on the *TODAY Show*, E!, *Inside Edition* and other broadcast shows in Washington, D.C., L.A., and beyond

I remember when Sydney made the important decision in 2018 to leave the security of her job at the *Daily Front Row*, where she was much loved, to branch out on her own. We were at Kings Theater in Brooklyn attending *Glamour Magazine*'s Women of the Year Awards Gala. She took me aside and said she wanted me to know she's leaving the *Daily* to branch out into other media and pursue being on-air. I wished her the best of luck, and said I was sorry to see her go. Little did I know what Sydney had in mind and how quickly she was going to make her mark.

Sydney's career trajectory coincided perfectly with the explosion of social media. Her energy and enthusiasm are contagious. I began following Sydney's Instagram account and I'm still in awe of how she keeps up with everything and how she does it all. She's on a plane several times a week, she's traveling to her gigs, she's packing and unpacking, she's up at the crack of dawn getting her hair and makeup done, she's in the gym with her trainer, and she's out at an event, party, trendy restaurant, or hosting an in-store event. And in between she's presenting live Instagram stories and posting her latest looks and outfits several times a day.

I am exhausted just from following her posts and her live feeds and the ever-changing wardrobe, accessories, hairstyles, and makeup looks. Sydney, I like you best au naturel with no makeup!

How she found the time to write this book is a mystery to me, but thankfully she did. Now her loyal followers and new fans can find out how she does it all. Now you too can also learn how to *Aim High*.

She learned that fashion can be empowering and that clothes alone won't make you look good . . . you have to feel good and that comes from the inside. In this book, she shares her tips on how you can use fashion to empower your life and make your dreams come true.

She'll suggest how you can purge and organize your closet and your shelves (hers display more handbags than books). Sydney will explain what "black tie optional" and "festive dressing" really mean and how to execute both from your own closet. She will also tell you how to dress for dating apps and how to live a fulfilled life you love no matter your fluctuating weight. You'll learn how to mix high and low . . . as her TV segments never include a garment over one hundred dollars. You'll read all about wearing shapewear, shopping vintage and resale, and packing all these clothes.

Aim High is fun to read, heart-filled, and accessible. It's a guide to finding your own voice and personal style and maximizing it to the hilt so you too can *Aim High* like Sydney Sadick did.

1.

FASHION 911

A woman is never sexier than when she is comfortable in her clothes.

—**Vera Wang**

I've always been comfortable and confident with my personal style and fashion choices, but let's face it, it's not this way for everyone. We all come in different shapes and sizes and have our own insecurities, but regardless, we strive to bring personal style out from within and present the best versions of ourselves to the world. While most people have some sort of an idea of how they want to look, making it a reality can be as challenging as overcoming your biggest fears. At a young age, I became the unofficial fashion EMT for my friends and family. No matter what the fashion 911 crises are, to this day they feel comfortable coming to me knowing I will solve their emergencies. That's what on-call doctors are for, right?! Last minute Bumble date with nothing to wear? No problem—a quick FaceTime call later and I'm virtually in my friend's closet and can assemble an outfit within minutes! She ends up looking effortless and fun, even though behind-the-scenes we just mad-dashed to create a great first impression. Going on a vacation and want to bring some new pieces but have a limited budget to spend? Easy! It's all about creatively repurposing your pieces and adding a few pops of new in ways that most wouldn't have the slightest clue how to nail.

Even after years of experience as *that* girl, never did I imagine I would be in a stranger's closet in Buckstown, Pennsylvania, doing my thing surrounded by the crew of *Hoda & Jenna* from NBC's *Today Show*.

Flashback to a boiling hot summer afternoon in late-August 2019. Tiptoeing around a lush flower garden surrounding a home in quaint Buckstown, Pennsylvania, I was terrified that sweat would ruin my makeup, camera-ready for the big surprise.

Today Show correspondent Donna Farizan led the way and I followed with a producer and two cameramen behind me. Her segment surprises selected viewers with a guest star visit to their home. The week prior, Mark Wahlberg visited an unsuspecting woman in Los Angeles. This week? Sydney Sadick on the opposite end of the country in Buckstown. This was my new reality, not a dream!

We were about to present Eileen, a die-hard *Today Show* fan, with a potentially life-changing gift. We hoped to solve her fashion emergency, which would potentially throw any woman into full-on panic mode: three weddings in multiple states within ONE WEEK! How is that even *possible*, you might be wondering, but it was very real for Eileen. And to make it even more of a challenge, each wedding was unique in location and dress code, requiring specific attention to make sure she was wearing something appropriate while still making a statement. Of course, you can imagine how expensive it would be to invest in three different looks within such a short period of time, especially when you're only likely to wear the clothes just for the occasion. Everything had to be perfect and planned. I'm normally super calm, but as we approached Eileen's front door, my heart started to race. I wanted to make sure I did everything right—for a woman I didn't even know. It was completely different than all those years spent helping friends and family. If I could solve Eileen's wardrobe dilemma and could help relieve her fashion *financial* burden, I would feel like I did my job. The financial piece was key, so she would still have money left over for wedding gifts and travel expenses. No easy task, for sure!

"What?! Sydney! Donna! At my house?!" Our cameras captured Eileen's shock as she looked back and forth between Donna and me on her front doorstep. She hugged us both, nearly in tears. Petite with silver hair, Eileen is a sixty-one-year-old personal trainer, wife, and mother. She wore a charcoal-grey triathlon t-shirt, athletic shorts, and rectangular glasses, a typical daily outfit completely within her fashion comfort zone.

"We heard through Sydney that you have three weddings to attend in one week, so we're bringing you to New York City, and Sydney will style you!" Donna said. These were magical words—a promise Eileen never expected to hear.

Eileen was speechless; she never believed that her wish would come true. Her usual day was going to work as a trainer in a basically calm environment. With that surprise, she was visibly thrilled and excited, especially because it was completely unexpected; hardly the day she'd planned.

Initially, Eileen reached out to me following my debut appearance on *Hoda & Jenna* in mid-July 2019. Impressed by my fashion ability, she went out of her comfort zone and wrote to me for help. She sent me an Instagram message with "high hopes" that I could help her with a fashion dilemma that made my mouth drop—and not much phases me.

The weddings included beachfront nuptials in Delaware; a winery wedding in Pennsylvania, followed by a reception in an outdoor pavilion; and a cocktail-attire wedding at the prestigious Franklin Institute Museum in Philadelphia. Eileen hoped to impress family and friends and wanted to look younger and stylish. She described a similar anxiety to what one feels before an upcoming high school reunion.

But this situation required knowledge of style and an assortment of clothing far beyond her experience or wallet. She didn't even know where to start. The stores in her area were limited and buying online was too risky due to the unreliable fit. On top of it all, coordinating everything together was overwhelming, and understandably so!

"My style is limited to t-shirts and gym shorts from the boy's department, because girls' sport shorts have no pockets," she wrote to me in an Instagram direct message. "I attended school in a uniform and never developed a sense of style! I need YOU!"

Eileen intuitively understood that I would try to help her. Whether or not the *Today Show* embarked on the project, it was my mission to assist. I assured Eileen that her multiple wedding dress emergency would be taken seriously. To our shared excitement, the *Today Show* agreed to document her wedding style journey, and before you knew it, we were rolling.

Eileen led our crew through her home and up to her closet. She graciously offered us drinks and even asked if she could take us to lunch. She exuded warmth. Few women open their closet to family, let alone strangers. A woman's closet is typically very personal, but Eileen was far from guarded. She welcomed our cameras into her private world and willingly shared this doorway into her life with our viewers.

She laughingly disclosed that her husband had more clothing than she did. Her entire wardrobe fit on one small rod in the lower half of their shared closet. Her fashion world consisted primarily of the comfortable outfits she trained in: leggings, shorts, and a few t-shirts. Eveningwear was limited to one tuxedo dress with a permanent food stain and a dark pantsuit that was frankly dated. "I told you, I've got nothing," she whispered.

Eileen clearly needed a creative solution. We reassured her that she had nothing to worry about—Eileen's problem was safely in my hands.

Think about her challenge: How to invest in affordable outfits for three equally important occasions within such a brief period—clothing she might never wear again. I'm sure you've faced similar fashion frustrations. My goal: To lift Eileen from her comfort zone, flatter her petite figure, and turn heads with affordable, reusable items.

An ordinary dress could be spiced up with different shoes, bags, and accessories, but at the end of the day, it would still be an ordinary dress. Then it came to me: What if one dress could be worn in multiple ways? It's something one rarely hears about—hardly a trending style at New York Fashion Week or at fast-fashion stores like Zara. But given my fashion network and experience, I knew such a dress existed. I Googled diverse word combinations: one dress for all occasions; multipurpose dresses; one dress that fits all. You name it, I entered it. As fate would have it, I finally found the Convertible Wrap Dress.

Translation: One dress that can be transformed into over one hundred styles! Yes, you read that correctly—over a hundred different ways! The dress could be worn with sleeves, sleeveless, backless, strapless, on and on, and is available in just about every color of the rainbow: Pastels, brights, neutral, and deep hues. Once you select your color, you can instantly transform the silhouette.

Eileen could wrap and accessorize for a distinctive look during the week of weddings and beyond. The best part? The price! Retailing for sixty-nine dollars, this truly affordable solution provided a stylish foundation for any fashion-worthy occasion.

While the dress was available in a plethora of colors, choosing the right option was no easy task. Although black is typically the safest choice, it's controversial for a wedding. I preferred a deeper fall tone because bright colors didn't seem appropriate for the season. I finally selected navy blue to illuminate her stunning blue eyes. The dress fit Eileen like a glove, each version accessorized with shoes, handbags, light outerwear, and jewelry based on the wedding setting.

Here's how I styled each look:

Beachfront: I wrapped the dress to its cap-sleeve silhouette, the most classic option, and paired it with transparent block-heeled sandals from Steve Madden—making it easier for Eileen to walk and socialize in the sand. I found a twenty-four dollar wooden-style bag from online retailer Boohoo, inspired by a high-end brand, which retails for hundreds of dollars. For the jewelry, I added dangling star earrings from Bauble Bar, my go-to destination for budget-friendly jewelry that surpasses expectations. The overall look was simple and fresh.

The Winery: To diversify the dress aesthetic, I transformed it into a halter neck silhouette. To allay Eileen's concern about feeling cold at the outdoor reception, I paired the dress with a reasonably priced Karl Lagerfeld cardigan in matching navy blue with white pipping. For accessories: A classic black kitten heel sandal from Steve Madden, a marble box bag embellished with a pearl closure from Anthropologie, and statement white drop earrings from Bauble Bar. The overall look was classic and preppy.

The Franklin Institute: A more formal venue, Eileen could bring on the glam with sparkle, shine, and sequins! So I wrapped the dress into a one-shoulder style, paired it with a metallic silver peep-toe heel from Steve Madden, a matching micro-bag from Urban Outfitters, a statement silver sequin shawl from Betsy Johnson, and crystal hanging earrings from Macy's.

The total cost of all the accessories for all three looks was under a hundred dollars, and they were sufficiently versatile to be comfortably used time and again.

"This is all yours!" I told Eileen after showing her my selections. The brands mentioned above, including the Convertible Wrap Dress, generously gifted their items to Eileen after hearing her story. The best part: *Today Show* viewers could quickly see how emergency fashion might be adapted to their needs. Of course, Eileen never imagined that it wouldn't cost her a penny.

But it was more than just receiving stunning clothes and accessories. With tears dotting her cheeks, she thanked us for expanding her comfort zone and helping her tap into the self-confidence that she always knew she possessed, but that she needed a boost to let shine through.

Just a few weeks later, Eileen met me at 30 Rockefeller Plaza in New York City, the home of the *Today Show*. It was the day before our live broadcast—rehearsal time. She arrived with her yoga instructor, also named Donna, a source of guidance and comfort for Eileen. She loves Donna's yoga class so much that she drives forty-five minutes weekly to attend. Donna reassured me that this was exactly what Eileen needed at this point in her life—she had faced many challenges and it was time for her to focus on herself.

To my delight, Eileen was already showing a new persona. Out of her athletic wear and into jeans paired with a plaid purple top, she proudly showed off her self-styled look. "I bought this yesterday! It looks like the purple plaid suit you just wore to New York Fashion Week!" Eileen exclaimed, referencing my outfit in an Instagram photo.

Eileen tried on the dress, and the wardrobe department examined how it functioned. This was critical because Eileen's appearance was unlike any prior *Today Show* segment. Our producers created a portable dressing room directly on stage for the show. The wardrobe team would help change Eileen into each look—on LIVE television. Talk about pressure—for everyone!

Eileen, trusting and with newfound confidence, was game. She was definitely ready for her fifteen minutes of national television fame. Eileen was in camera-ready hair and makeup bright and early the following morning. Although a bit nervous backstage, she was also overjoyed. Eileen looked forward to meeting Hoda and guest host Meredith Viera, who was filling in for Jenna while she was out on maternity leave.

I told Eileen that if she felt nervous during the process, to just look at me. I had her back. She was not alone. We were in this together.

The segment opened with the "Donna's Door Knock" video, featuring our surprise at Eileen's home. Moments later, Eileen appeared on stage, proudly modeling the beach ensemble in front of millions of viewers across the nation. Her face glowed and she radiated confidence. She then returned to the make-shift mini dressing room behind a black curtain and changed into her winery wedding dress in less than two minutes. Eileen was now confident in her skin, and it started with her new clothes. While there was insufficient time to showcase the glamorous Franklin Institute ensemble, the *Today Show* posted a photo on its website.

Once the segment wrapped, we snapped a fan photo with Hoda, Meredith, and both Donnas that would forever memorialize the moment. Eileen presented me with a touching and beautiful gift of cut crystal wine glasses. Unnecessary, but they will forever remind me of her joy. Eileen departed the studio with her glamorous wardrobe, as well as an unexpected gift of nearly one hundred new makeup products from Urban Decay so that she could be camera-ready for the weddings. We hugged and said our goodbyes. It was hard to believe it was over, but our shared memories will not be forgotten. Eileen was clearly ready to take on the weddings and any future fashion crises that come her way.

Eileen's journey reflects a notion I've always associated with fashion: how our clothing choices indicate more about who we are than we realize. The way you dress is a reflection of your inner self. Clothing can truly impact how you think, how you feel, and how others perceive you. Your daily wardrobe choices affect your relationships, the people you attract, being hired or not for a job, and your career, to name a few. I've lived through this.

Fashion helps set the tone for your "on-stage" life appearances. I spend quite a bit of time curating my daily looks, even if I'm not preparing for a public appearance. A drugstore run or trip to the grocery store is just as important as a big event. You never know who you'll see or meet. Trust me! I can't tell you how many times I have run out for something inconsequential and ran into a potential boyfriend, an ex-boyfriend, a former work colleague, or a hot celebrity like Jake Gyllenhaal having coffee at my favorite neighborhood spot. A few run-ins like these and you'll think further about running out in your comfy sweats, dirty hair, and no makeup.

Helping others to look and feel their best—and indeed, to exceed their own expectations—is a heartwarming achievement. Helping *you* fulfill your personal fashion dreams and requirements at an affordable cost for every life scenario is absolutely priceless. I believe it's important to get to a place where putting together an outfit becomes second nature once you create a base wardrobe foundation and then you can add seasonal trends or special occasion needs. You truly need to know yourself and how you want to be perceived by others, as personal style truly comes from within.

2.

MY FASHION LOVE STORY

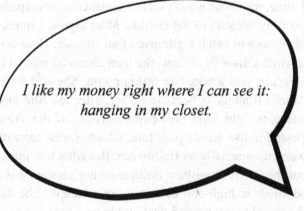

I like my money right where I can see it: hanging in my closet.

—**Carrie Bradshaw**

Growing up as a '90s kid, *Sex and the City* was in its prime. Definitely not appropriate to watch as a pre-teen, but at that time, my focus wasn't on the romance or sexcapades. I was intrigued fully because of the fashion. Most nights, I snuck into my mom's bedroom to catch a glimpse of an episode. How could I not be obsessed?! Carrie Bradshaw, the lead character played by Sarah Jessica Parker, was a bonafide fashion icon. She still is! I learned who Manolo Blahnik is because of her, after all. She made fashion statements right from the opening credits of the show, where she appeared in that iconic pink tutu, which is now recreated by so many women, especially on Halloween. But what was most admirable about the Carrie Bradshaw fashion-loving persona was how she shopped all these high-end designers on a budget. She did everything she could to get a good deal and have a piece of her favorite designers hanging right in her closet. She knew every sample sale and every salesperson who could give her the lowdown on sales (remember when Andy Cohen played the Barney's shoes salesman?). She was a true fashion insider with all of the right knowledge and contacts. Now, ironically, I re-watch the series for the very reason I wasn't allowed to watch it in the first place—the dating (I'll say "dating" here to keep it PG) lessons are still very relevant today, twenty years later. As the saying goes, life comes full circle. And to this day, women are still obsessed with her outfits and recreating them in modern ways.

Carrie Bradshaw was my first fashion love, but so many other influential characters, celebrities, and others have shaped my love of clothes, accessories, makeup, and shoes.

If Carrie was my first, Rihanna was my second. She made a splash in the music world right around 2010 when I was coming into my own as a high schooler. Like most Hollywood stars, she always seemed so unapproachable. But little did I know, that was about to change.

It was fall and I had just returned to NYC after completing a summer program at Harvard University where I launched my first blog called Style Solutions. Now that I was home and the blog was no longer a school project but a budding business venture, I was ready to take it to the next level. A new idea hit me, thanks to my mom's Sunday ritual of reading the *New York Times*. Scanning the paper, a Barnes & Noble advertisement for an upcoming event stood out: a book signing by Rihanna. Who would have thought the hottest singer of the moment would be at our local bookstore?

Rihanna was on a book tour for her new autobiography and was doing a book signing at the Barnes & Noble Fifth Avenue flagship. I've always been a huge Rihanna fan—her songs dominated my iPod playlists. I thought to myself, *what if I attended the appearance, asked her for a quote, took a picture together, and blogged about it?* Rihanna had reached superstardom, so I knew this could generate a lot of clicks. I anticipated a huge crowd and wondered how I could actually make it happen.

Then I realized there was an even bigger problem—the signing began at two in the afternoon. Translation: during school hours. Celebrities generate enormous turnouts for personal appearances in NYC. I had to arrive early enough to avoid the massive line or at best, be at the beginning of this line.

Luckily, I had Spanish class during that hour and was close with my teacher, Senorita Allub. She was a big supporter of my Style Solutions ambitions, but I was still nervous to ask if I could skip her class to attend the signing. I had never requested such a favor from a teacher before and was frankly terrified.

As fate would have it, she said yes, and I headed to the signing the following day. The line was even worse than I'd expected. It wrapped around an entire city block and well over 150 people were waiting. I stood toward the end of the line. Arriving thirty minutes in advance clearly wasn't enough to beat the crowds. I have my father's patience, which is slim to none, and it was a freezing fall afternoon. I wasn't dressed appropriately at all—a tannish nude blouse over black leggings and a leather jacket.

Nearly two hours later, despite the poor outfit choice and even poorer patience, I made it inside the store. I was sure they would stop letting people in at a certain point, so just getting through the door was a major accomplishment. Excited to execute my idea, I was on a professional mission that would hopefully launch my new career.

Soon, I was up close enough to see Rihanna's outfit. She wore a short sleeve multicolored floral dress in punchy hues with pops of white and green. I should not have been surprised, but that day her hair was bright red, and her nails were painted purple. She was definitely recognizable as a shimmering star. Rihanna's team was moving fans quickly. But to be honest, a little too quickly for my plan. I intended to ask her a question and request that she write the answer—instead of her autograph—in her book.

The moment was here. Before I could say anything, Rhianna said, "Hi! What's your name for the book?" A little nervous, but filled with excitement, I said, "I'm Sydney Sadick, but instead of writing my name, could you please write down your favorite fashion trend this year?" She just looked at me. She didn't even answer. For a split second, I was a bit concerned. I'd asked her something that the 149 people ahead of me didn't ask—obviously rare.

I couldn't tell what she was thinking or writing. I was simultaneously getting my phone ready to give to the person behind, begging her to take my picture with Rihanna. Without asking, Rihanna put the book down and leaned across the table to smile for my picture. She sensed it coming.

I left beaming with excitement that we spoke, and I actually had proof with a photo that we met. I nervously opened the book to see if she acted on my request. The front page was inked in a giant gold scribble that read Rihanna, and at the top of the page, she'd written "Hair Accessories."

OMG. Rhianna answered my question! Thrilled, I phoned my parents to tell them the news! Rihanna answered MY question! I thought to myself, do I now have the potential to be a news reporter? I didn't ask a question that received a "yes" or "no," but a very specific answer. I rushed home to write about my afternoon. A short and sweet post that featured my Rihanna quote and a photo of us together. Within hours, it generated thousands of clicks.

I knew I was onto something. And Rihanna's two-word answer would be the beginning of my fashion reporting journey.

Looking back, it's wild to think how the decision of going to Harvard for a summer instead of summer camp—the more typical path of my friends—essentially changed everything for me.

The fall of my sophomore year, an email arrived from my mom with the subject line: "About Harvard Summer Program." The courses described resonated with me, and I was excited about the prospect of something new. But I was also a bit worried. I had never slept away from home without my family. No exaggeration. Summer camp in the wilderness without cell phones? No thank you. Weekend sleepovers with friends? Didn't I see enough of them during the school week?! Case in point: Not my thing.

My parents were convinced that a decent college would not accept me without "away from home" experiences. They feared I would earn negative marks without cross-country teen trips or foreign adventures featuring altruistic activities like saving animals or volunteering in an international hospital. Truthfully, I've always been a homebody and was comfortable in my world. I was developing my own skincare brand, Color My Destiny, and sitting on beauty panels at *Teen Vogue*. Why would sleeping in a bed that was not mine and being separated from my family help me get into college?

Nevertheless, I was admitted to the Harvard summer program and off I went for a six-week Cambridge adventure in a dorm room without air-conditioning (the first thing I discovered during my

Google search.) Although nervous, I thought of Elle Woods in *Legally Blonde*. Elle loved Harvard. Sure, it was Harvard Law School, but in the movie, she made it seem like the Disney World of academia. She brought her flare, her style, and she even met a hot teacher's assistant and married him. Fairytale vibes, indeed.

I selected two college level courses in journalism that sounded fun. How poorly could I do in this type of class? At the same time, if I didn't get a good grade, it would seem like a waste. On the first day of summer school, Professor Martha Bebinger, an esteemed writer for the *Boston Globe*, instructed us to create a blog on any topic. There were relatively few high school bloggers in 2010. I didn't know what to do, how to do it, or what the subject matter should be. What in the world was I going to write about?

I spent hours in the Harvard library trying to come up with a topic and then suddenly it hit me: a fashion blog. I lived and breathed clothes and shoes. My grandma and mom started me on this path with beautiful onesies, and my fashion sense evolved from there. I visited nearly every clothing store in Cambridge (research!), took pictures, and posted about different trends and my favorite finds. While my hometown, New York City, is the fashion capital of the world, this was no easy task in Cambridge. Finally, at nearly one in the morning on a hot, humid night, Style Solutions was born.

When I returned to class the next morning, I was literally the only student out of over thirty classmates who showed up with a finished product. I was shocked because I took the assignment very seriously and would never return to class without my work. My professor was pleasantly surprised and sufficiently impressed that she asked me to present my site to the class . . . on day two! My classmates were into it. They liked the name, they liked the content, and I was having the best time writing and creating it. I was sending my fashion opinions and photos into the universe. By the time the summer program ended, the blog had taken on a life of its own.

I left Harvard with new friends and a new passion: *writing* about fashion. Style Solutions returned to New York with me, and I embraced it with a full-fledged Empire State of Mind. And speaking of warm memories, I even dated the hottest guy in my program.

He played guitar and sang to me—enough to make me swoon after attending a girl's school for twelve very long years. But like Carrie Bradshaw's love life, things got a little more complex after that.

Armed with Style Solutions, a short-lived summer romance, and a killer Rihanna story, things really did take off from there. I was interviewing a different personality, celeb, or designer every week: Lauren Conrad, Carmen Electra, Diane Von Furstenberg, and the original Charlie's Angel, Jaclyn Smith. I was a high school student, but somehow that didn't stop these names from speaking with me. I hustled and constantly networked, pitching myself and story ideas so I could be granted interviews. I also started getting invited to fashion shows; I attended my first New York Fashion Week at sixteen. Sitting front row next to the budding bloggers of that time and celebs literally felt like a dream.

Simultaneously, I realized it would be fun to have real-life internship experience at a media company, and ended up landing a gig at the *Daily Front Row*, the long-running bible of New York Fashion Week, where I essentially did what I was doing for Style Solutions but in a bigger way. I was able to balance the two throughout college, which helped shape what I wanted to do even further down the line. As the old saying goes, life is a journey—and my career has definitely been one.

3.

MET GALA CAMP

Create your own style . . . let it be unique for yourself and yet identifiable for others.

—Anna Wintour

MET GALA CAMP

W hen "Camp" was initially announced as the theme for the 2019 Met Gala, confusion struck not just among the public, but among seasoned fashion insiders. When you hear "Camp," you probably think of summer camp or camouflage, right? Only natural. It wasn't long before rumors began circulating, so I quickly reached out to my "in-the-know" fashion industry friends for their thoughts.

I texted my friend Romeo Hunte, a New York-based designer whose creations have appeared on Michelle Obama; New York Fashion Week creator Fern Mallis; and Zach Weiss, a writer for *Vogue*. Ultimately, no one could explain what this theme really signified. All three fashion insiders were cautious. Mistakes simply could not be made with Anna Wintour at the helm of the event. That's when I realized that the only way to figure out what "Camp" meant in Anna Wintour's dictionary was to get inside the press conference. Luckily, I planned ahead and was able to land a highly coveted ticket to the media briefing and the Gala itself, which was later that evening.

The morning of the opening press conference, I walked into the Costume Institute—the museum section spearheaded by *Vogue*'s editor-in-chief and Conde Nast artistic director, Anna Wintour—with a racing heart. Who else would be here? What would the exhibit look like? Could I get an inside scoop on the Gala? The anticipation was thrilling. Even more thrilling: the morning after the Gala, I was booked for my debut segment on E! News where I'd show viewers how they could achieve wearable versions of the most iconic and over-the-top looks from the Met Gala red carpet, all on a budget.

The "Who's Who" of the fashion industry filled the seats around me: my friend Fern (of course), designer Zandra Rhodes, *Vogue* head honchos, and other big names from top fashion publications. Wintour arrived promptly at 10 a.m. with her entourage and we all looked to her outfit for clues about the theme, "Camp." She wore her signature sunglasses, multicolor necklaces, and a green printed maxi dress. Andrew Bolton, curator of the Costume Institute, who recommends the annual exhibit theme, and Gucci's Creative Director Alessandro Michele (Gucci sponsored the exhibit) joined Wintour. Together, they presented this year's exhibit concept to the select group of editors and fashion legends.

A red carpet event is the easiest place for a celebrity to demonstrate how their style is a visual representation of who they are on the inside. We learn so much by watching their fashion choices and how they confidently show them off at what's become the most coveted invite on the global fashion stage.

In the weeks leading up to the Gala, I watched from 5th Avenue as a set-up team worked diligently to quickly and efficiently arrange *the* major New York City social event of the year. Just getting a glimpse from the outside is thrilling and makes you feel like a part of it, even if you don't have the privilege of an invite. Builders finally finished putting up a gigantic light pink tent that read "CAMP: Notes on Fashion," perched over the steps that lead up to the Metropolitan Museum of Art on the Upper East Side of Manhattan. It was pure eye candy.

While every day is special at the iconic museum, this event was on steroids. The Met Gala is the most sought-after ticket of the year. The 2019 event was no different, featuring the high fashion art of the Anna Wintour Costume Center. As an Instagram-obsessed millennial, I quickly took a photo in front of the tent and posted it to my Instagram feed. The likes started pouring in, and my followers wondered what I was up to and how this year's Met Gala would compare to the ones before.

The setting of the Met Gala, held every year on the first Monday of May, is where moments are created and become talked about for years to come. Some of the most dished-about moments, to refresh you:

- In 2018, 2 Chainz proposed to Kesha Ward.
- In the same year, Katy Perry's Versace outfit, complete with angel wings, was so outrageous that she had to be transported there in an open, roof-less Rolls Royce. This served two purposes: it fit her and her entire outfit *and* enabled the public to see.
- In 2017, Jaden Smith carried his own dreadlock—new accessory trend, anyone? Actor Jared Leto nodded to this in 2019 by carrying a mannequin of his own head. Remember?!
- Also in 2017, the viral bathroom photo: the party seemed to be taking place more in the bathroom than at the gala when Kylie Jenner broke the internet by posting a viral Instagram photo of herself with sisters Kim Kardashian and Kendall Jenner, A$AP Rocky, Luka Sabbat, *Moonlight* star Ashton Sanders, Paris Jackson, Lily Aldridge, the reclusive Frank Ocean, Sean "Diddy" Combs, model Slick Woods, and actress Brie Larson. This prompted Wintour to reinforce a "no selfie" rule in 2018.

Themes have included: "Heavenly Bodies: Fashion and the Catholic Imagination;" "Rei Kawakubo/Comme des Garcons: Art of the In-Between;" "Manus x Machina: Fashion in the Age of Technology;" and "China: Through the Looking Glass."

To put it in broader turns, it's the Super Bowl of fashion. Everyone who's anyone attends the annual fundraising gala. The list changes every year, but it always attracts the biggest names in film, music, Broadway, fashion, and modeling. Kim Kardashian, Kanye West, Gigi and Bella Hadid, Beyoncé, Diddy, Elon Musk, and Celine Dion (she sang to me one year on the carpet) have all attended, among a plethora of others. Every person invited must be approved by Anna Wintour and are expected to choose outfits (also subject to Wintour's approval) that match the theme of the exhibit. Each and every detail is critical and highly strategized. For top designers, it's probably their most high-pressured week of the year.

Wintour annually taps a lineup of co-chairs to spearhead the gala. For "Camp," she enlisted Lady Gaga, Alessandro Michele, Harry Styles, and Serena Williams.

At the press conference, Andrew Bolton explained that the exhibition was framed around writer Susan Sontag's 1964 essay "Notes on Camp," which details different ideologies and connotations of the word "Camp." The highly influential essay arguably introduced "Camp" to a wider audience. Bolton noted in his speech that "Camp embraces irony, humor, parody, pastiche, artifice, theatricality, excess, extravagance, nostalgia, and exaggeration" and that the theme was "very relevant to the cultural conversation" going on in the world. The same can be said about fashion as a whole. Fashion embraces the intersection of extravagance and nostalgia and furthers cultural conversation while also serving a substantial role in our daily lives.

Often you need to see something—not just hear about it—to fully understand what is seemingly complex. Following the conference, we were allowed to preview the exhibit for the first time. Walking in, my face lit up. It was like the Candy Land of fashion and totally opposite of what everyone seemed to have envisioned, including myself. Clothing from a range of designers was on display in an architecturally dreamy set-up in multiple rooms featuring extremely glamorous, over the top, highly constructed silhouettes. Drama, embellishments, and tons and tons of colors enveloped the room with designs from Valentino, Off-White, Schiaparelli, Moschino, Thom Browne, Dior, and many more. Many designers stood in front of their creations and took pictures for all to see. It was all very high fashion; very impressive; very Anna Wintour.

After listening to the press conference and seeing the exhibit, it was easier to grasp what we could expect to see later in the night on the red carpet. My predictions included puff sleeves, elaborate embellishments, and bright colors, to name a few.

With only a few hours to spare before the carpet began, it was critical to select my outfit for my debut segment on E! News, which we were filming the next morning. I ordered a few options online based on what I imagined "Camp" to look like, but I still had to make my final choice.

I kept debating how I should dress. Should I go with something more wearable and relatable, something that screamed "red carpet glam," or something in between? Then it hit me: I'd found a dress during my online search from a brand called Rotate. It was a metallic orange lamé dress with a puff shoulder. It was in the sweet spot between wearable and red carpet aspirational. It would be perfect for my debut segment.

I quickly went into glam-mode. First, a manicure that incorporated the orange hue of my dress. Then, I sent makeup and hair inspiration to Glamsquad, an app that coordinates my makeup and hair appointments. I love that I'm able to request the same stylists every time and upload celebrity photos of the look I'm hoping to achieve. This was no ordinary event and my look had to be perfect from head to toe. I didn't know if this was going to be the right choice, but it was just a gut feeling that struck me.

In past years, I reported—or I "worked the red carpet" in fashion lingo—on this iconic event as a writer and editor for *Daily Front Row,* interviewing celebrity attendees about what it's like attending such a seminal event, their extravagant outfits, and other hot topics. *Daily Front Row* is in print during New York Fashion Week (twice a year) and then during the summer for their Hamptons edition.

While working the red carpet as an editorial reporter in 2016 and 2017 was a dream in itself, I told myself that the next time I covered the Met Gala in any capacity, it must be televised.

In 2019, it finally happened.

My very first fashion segment for E! News would be my biggest reporting challenge yet. Within just a few hours between the evening Gala and my 7 a.m. call time the next morning, I had to take notes on what the celebs wore, find a duplicate version at a practical price for viewers to purchase, make sure I reached stores before closing since it was during the evening, send all my picks to the producer to approve, and be ready to film with the models dressed perfectly. No time for errors, that was for certain.

The clock struck 7:00 p.m. The red carpet—which was really a pink carpet—was just about to begin, as was my work. My mom and I were in a taxi headed to midtown along Fifth Avenue, where stores like Zara, GUESS?, H&M, and Topshop were located. I arranged to pull clothing from these stores for my segment—each was expecting me, and knew I was in a tight time crunch. I had the E! red carpet coverage livestreamed on my iPhone so I could watch in the moment and determine which looks would be the strongest to mimic for my segment.

Anna Wintour and her daughter Bee Shafer were the first people to walk down the carpet, as per tradition.

Next came who I knew was going to be the showstopper of the evening: Lady Gaga. And what LOOKS they were! Yes, plural. She didn't just wear one show-stopping outfit. She chose to make four outfit changes, crafting an entrance that would go down in red carpet history. Her red carpet ensemble inspired my first look on E! the next morning.

LOOK 1: LADY GAGA FOR A LOW PRICE

Lady Gaga appeared alongside designer and pal Brandon Maxwell, first stepping onto the steps in a bright pink, oversized gown. She was accompanied by six dancers dressed in tuxedos, carrying black umbrellas. Her first look was paired with bright pink matching lipstick and eyelashes that were tipped with metallic gold. Next came her second look: Maxwell untied and unzipped the pink gown to reveal a black strapless ball gown. It was all fashion and theater.

And then came the bright pink maxi slip dress. There was a hint of black lingerie underneath, and she topped it off with props like an oversized cell phone, black embellished sunglasses, platform heels, and a diamond necklace. Finally, the grand finale: the pink slip dress came off and Gaga strutted her stuff in sparkly lingerie, platform shoes, and fishnet stockings. It was amazing. Hollywood entertainment and fashion truly united.

It became clear that this was going to be one of the most talked about looks of the night, so it was critical to make a wearable version that took inspiration from it for my segment. I found an identical pink slip dress from Zara that retailed for forty-nine dollars and layered it with a patent leather black sleeveless trench coat that covered it so when on the show, viewers wouldn't notice the model was wearing something else underneath until opening it. Under the pink dress, I found little black lingerie for the model to wear underneath, just like Gaga, which peek-a-booed through the dress.

The look was complete with fishnet sock boots from Schutz, encrusted with crystals, and like Gaga, hot pink lipstick. While Met Gala looks can cost up to hundreds of thousands of dollars, my version came to approximately two hundred.

LOOK 2: SERENA WILLIAMS FOR A STEAL

Next came Serena Williams, who was a vision in a bright yellow floral embellished Atelier Versace gown with matching Off White x Nike sneakers. She shined. It was a moment. My mom and I ran around Topshop looking for a yellow dress—not a color you see around stores every day. Somehow, an adorable dress in the bright yellow with a similar fabric appeared. It was perfect. But the look wouldn't be complete without sneakers. With our Topshop bags, we sprinted over to Nike to find a pair of similar kicks. We found them—it was a win.

LOOK 3: ASHLEY GRAHAM AT A BARGAIN

I needed two more looks for my segment. Since Gucci sponsored the exhibit, it felt appropriate to have a Gucci look in my segment. Model Ashley Graham showed off some major glamour in head-to-toe Gucci: a red and green blazer dress with patchwork embellishments, crystal covered stockings and stocking boots, mismatched earrings, and stacks of Gucci hairclips placed along her ponytail. We next ran over to Zara.

Bustling through racks and racks of clothing appeared a green and white tweed blazer, which I had to transform into a dress. I purchased up a few sizes so that it would fit our model more like a dress. It was perfect and retailed for just eighty-nine dollars, a great deal.

The hair moment had to be replicated, too—luckily, I always keep stacks of embellished clips from Amazon handy. They topped off my affordable version of the outfit, along with metallic silver mule sandals from Schutz, and quirky crystal pineapple earrings, also from Zara, to give it that element of pizzazz.

LOOK 4: GIGI HADID AT HALF PRICE

The carpet was still streaming live on my iPhone, when supermodel Gigi Hadid appeared in a dazzling white, silver, and gold streaked sequin catsuit with a matching coat adorned with feathers, and even a matching, futuristic headpiece. The ensemble was designed by her date for the evening, Michael Kors. This was definitely Hadid's most showstopping look, marking her sixth time attending the Met Gala.

Everything about her look was perfect, and it definitely needed to make a splash on my segment. My mom and I didn't recall seeing sequins at any of the stores we were at previously—it was May, after all. We were standing on Fifth Avenue figuring out what to do. We walked about a block and came across Victoria's Secret. There, in the window, was my golden ticket: A white and gold sequin bodysuit and pant set that screamed Gigi Hadid's outfit. The set retailed for 128 dollars and truly looked like the wearable version of Gigi's look. I paired it with a white blazer, metallic gold pumps, and a statement metallic necklace.

By 9:30 p.m., the carpet ended, and all of my budget-friendly versions of the Met Gala looks were ready to go for my E! News shoot the next morning. At 10:30 p.m., four models showed up to my apartment for a fitting to make sure everything fit, which it did, and we were in great shape.

When the segment aired, viewers were shocked by how similar my looks were to the celebrity outfits—and how my "in-theme" orange Rotate dress so closely resembled model Kendall Jenner's orange feathered ensemble of the night. With my help, viewers from all backgrounds could replicate the Met Gala red carpet fashion for affordable prices.

Being selective with fabric, texture, patterns, color, and silhouettes all helped me achieve these similar looks for lower prices.

Lower-priced fast-fashion stores often use these high-end courtier designers for inspiration. When you learn to pick up on those special details and find ways to emulate them with consumer-friendly brands, it can make a big difference in achieving the *perception* of high fashion.

My debut E! segment was only the beginning. I didn't know it at the time, but this planted the seed of my own fashion mantra that continues to ring true today: Fashion is not about how much money you spend to achieve a great look. It's about finding inspiration that speaks to you, shopping in stores with great merchandise at prices that make you comfortable, and creatively pulling it all together. This is how you make a fashion statement.

4.

CAFETERIA CREW MAKEOVER

Clothes mean nothing until someone lives in them.

—Marc Jacobs

CAFETERIA CREW
MAKEOVER

I entered the doors of Milburn High School in Morristown, New Jersey as a very dressed down version of myself. Usually when on assignment for a television segment, my hair and makeup are professionally done, my outfit is a major fashion statement styled from head-to-toe, and I'm camera ready. But not this time. I was tasked to be incognito so I wouldn't give away a special surprise. My hair was slicked up in a messy ponytail; not an ounce of makeup could be found on my face; and my outfit was nondescript: a simple black sweater, black jeans, a leather jacket, and boots. I was trying to look unlike myself, the "fashion expert," as much as possible. This was my version of dressing undercover.

I was on a mission to get the clothing and shoe sizes of eight cafeteria workers at the high school for a national television segment. I had to pull it all together in just a little over twenty-four hours, a tight turnaround but what's commonly expected by television standards. The *Inside Edition* team called on me to give makeovers to the cafeteria staffers for a segment on the show. The cafeteria staff is such an important group for any school and often everyone is too busy to show their appreciation for their hard work.

When I heard about the topic, I was ecstatic. It was a great feel-good spin on a classic makeover segment, and it's something I knew could be fun for the women involved. And if you weren't paying close attention earlier, let's back up: this wasn't one makeover, but eight makeovers! I'd given multiple makeovers on other broadcasts, but normally two to three at the most—never to this many women, never all at one time, and certainly never without their specific size details. This time around, I had to basically guess their sizes by visually looking at them. But I love a good challenge—I was up for it.

As I observed the women from a distance, I noticed their different ages, sizes, varying personalities, and even life circumstances based on their physical appearances. The little information I received before I arrived told me their ages ranged mid-twenties to early-seventies, and everyone had a different story. One woman had just lost her husband earlier in the year and was trying to adjust to her new life and financial situation. Another woman recently had knee surgery and wore a cast. Some of the women were single and looking to get into dating. Others were loud personalities who didn't hold back, while one twenty-something, for example, was quiet and shy.

Getting the *sizes* of these women would be no easy task. I knew they would likely find it weird that a random girl they'd never seen before would come up to them asking such a personal question. So, the *Inside Edition* crew created a plan for how we'd introduce ourselves, which was coordinated with the school's administration. That way, everyone was on the same page. We also had to get b-roll during this visit (extra visual footage to use for the package), so it was critical for our "disguise" to be perfect.

The head of the cafeteria introduced the two show producers, a camera man, and me to the women as employees of the corporate food company that ran the cafeteria operations (an outside group). He went on to tell them that we were filming a commercial for the company. They didn't seem to suspect anything. Check!

After we got the b-roll, my producer told the ladies that they would be getting new uniforms—also known as my secret moment to get the sizes! The women looked surprised, and definitely a little suspicious. We had no idea what they were thinking, but it looked like they could sense that something was up. However, I don't think they suspected the extreme surprise that was to come.

Eventually, one of the women caved and told me her size (that was Debbie, mid-fifties and definitely the leader of the pack) and luckily the rest followed. If Debbie was game, the rest of the ladies would follow. But it was tricky because the uniforms definitely had more of a comfy fit—baggy and oversized—since they are designed for ease at work. How this size would translate into my clothing selections was a major concern and required some creative thinking.

I took mental notes on what I really thought were these women's true sizes. I also snapped some pictures during the b-roll filming to refer back to when putting together the outfit selections. I was in full-on fashion investigative reporter mode. The women also made small suggestions for their preferences, which I jotted down discreetly. "Make sure the pants have stretch!" said Jenna. "We're not going to be in dresses, are we?!" asked Lisa. These comments gave me major insights into what these women were looking for in clothing. It's the little details and preparation in high-pressure moments like these that help to make sure everything goes smoothly.

Driving back to Manhattan from Morristown, I reflected on the women I'd met. Many had worked at the school for over a decade, preparing lunches with tons of options for over a thousand students every day. They were creative, stocking everything from salad bars to a hot meal station, to prepackaged sandwiches, yogurt, fruit, sweets, and more. It was really impressive and included far more choices than when I was in high school. Definitely no easy task. Each woman had her specific assigned job—Vicky, Joanne, and Sandra primarily cleaned the dishes, Debbie and Bettie ran the cash register, and Chloe, Joanne, and Irene served the food. After watching them for a few hours, it was clear how hard they worked and how much they truly cared about their students. The cafeteria ladies had a special familiarity with the high schoolers and even knew many of their food preferences. It was obvious to me that these women didn't do much for themselves and always gave to others, both at home and at work. They certainly deserved a special treat.

Now that I had their names, sizes, age ranges, and photos, it was time to pick out their looks. Often people ask me how I do this. It's like an artist starting with an empty canvas and only ideas. I first thought it would be best to limit the stores. I normally go to dozens of stores and brands for one segment but consolidating made sense in this case. Macy's and Burlington kindly agreed to lend clothing and accessories for the ladies to wear for the segment and, since it was early December, to gift the clothing to these women as a holiday surprise!

While the producers and I agreed that we wanted there to be a noticeable transformation, it was also important to pick outfits the women would feel comfortable in. Nothing too over the top. Rather, elevated glamour through silhouettes that put them at ease. It was also critical to keep each woman's age in mind, as well as their body type. Going through the floors of Macy's, rack after rack, I selected an array of dresses, pants, tops, and jackets: primarily darker fall hues with pops of metallic and sparkle, since we were moving into the holiday season. For Chloe, the girl in her twenties, I wanted to show off her youth and go with a colorful faux fur jacket with a matching striped sweater and jeans—an easy day-to-night look that she could wear when not working. Jernelle was in her thirties and married, so I wanted to give her a fun date-night outfit: a satin pencil skirt in burgundy with a sleeveless turtleneck top and sparkly denim jacket to add a little edge. For the more mature women in the group, sticking to flattering, stretchy black pants with colorful tops would do the trick. Every look could be transformed from day to night, and the pieces could all be worn separately in many different ways. The women could truly make use of the items long beyond the televised moment.

Next stop was Burlington, my hub for accessories. Accessories can truly make or break an outfit. While clothing is the foundation, accessories take a look from good to great. I left with bags and bags of selections of clutches, cross bodies, totes, and more. The shoes were definitely the biggest challenge, as I had mainly selected heels—low heels, but nonetheless, not flat—which most of the women rarely wore. They told me they always selected shoes based on comfort, not fashion, so I wanted to show them how they could find shoes that were fashionable and still comfortable, making them a go-to accessory to elevate their looks.

With just a few hours to spare until the big surprise, my mind was racing. Would the clothes fit? Would the women like my choices? Were my picks aligned with their taste? Would they allow me to make them over? I was up all night contemplating and putting together the looks for each person, styling them with last-minute oversized earrings and bracelets to add that element of glamour that I knew would make these outfits look extra special. I laid each look out on my living room floor, took pictures of them so I knew which look was for each woman, and packed them into individual garment bags which would then be given to the women back at the school.

Before I knew it, the alarm clock on my phone buzzed and 5 a.m. struck. I was off to school—Milburn High School. This time, I was totally camera ready in a plaid power suit, sparkly makeup, and freshly blown-out hair. My mom came with me, and we arrived with eight hanging bags organized with each woman's outfit and matching accessories.

Students stared as we walked through the halls around the time they were arriving for their classes. They were in what you'd imagine teenagers would wear to school—mainly jeans and leggings with t-shirts and hoodies. We definitely looked a bit out of place! Eventually we made it to the back room of the cafeteria that was used to prepare the food. The aroma of mac and cheese and chicken fingers permeated the hallways.

The producers from *Inside Edition* had also set up hair and makeup appointments for the ladies to give them a morning of pampering, which they announced as the women walked through the door for work. This was exciting for most, although a few were uncomfortable with being glammed up by strangers. Assuming this was the extent of the surprise, for the most part they were thrilled! Giggling and having fun together, they complimented each other's new hairstyles (some straightened, other's waved or curled) and gave suggestions to their artists as to how they liked their makeup done. Some of the women opted for bold red or pink lipstick, while others were excited for statement cat-eye eyeliner.

From this, I learned that no matter what type of life you live, women have their own idea of how they should look and are very set in their ways. To introduce change is difficult and it often takes a life-altering event to trigger it: a family death, a serious accident, or divorce. To be able to guide women to help themselves is something that will never get old. Sometimes all it takes is a little push from a friend, or in this case, an expert who they can trust.

The biggest part of the surprise was yet to come, and my anticipation was building.

When the women were done with their hair and makeup, their boss revealed that they were going to be on television. Introducing myself, I explained that I'm an on-air fashion expert and would be styling them with head-to-toe fashion from Macy's and Burlington. I doubt even one of them recognized me from the day before because my look was a true transformation. Leading them into yet another room where the garment bags of clothing were placed on a rack, I also explained that Macy's and Burlington were gifting them the outfits and accessories.

The women were absolutely shocked! They really felt special. Naturally, they were simultaneously a little uncomfortable with all of the attention. Initially we were going to hand out the garment bags in an organized fashion and assist them in getting in the clothes one by one. But they were so excited that they hurried over to their respective bag, each one labeled with their name on it.

I watched anxiously, as the sizes were truly a guestimate (though I'd made sure that I had multiple options, just in case). Of course, I was also concerned about whether they would like my selections and not be embarrassed to wear them since they would be wearing them for the world to see on national television. Lots of pressure was mounting for ME! Every woman was pleasantly surprised with what I selected for them. It was so much fun watching them take an item out and show it to their colleagues, knowing I picked something so beautiful and unique to them.

I think the most special moment was when they actually tried on the clothes and looked in the mirror and saw this new version of themselves. I watched one of the more mature women in the group, Bettie, put on a pair of heels for the first time in years—she didn't even think she would be able to walk in them. But she very much did, and was so excited to see how great she looked when gazing at

35

herself in the mirror. All of the women appeared how I envisioned they would and on top of it, each outfit fit!

With their new clothes on, it was time to surprise the over a thousand students waiting in the lunchroom. Steven Fabian, an *Inside Edition* reporter, used the loudspeaker to explain who we were and what we had planned.

The women entered the room in a straight line like a runway fashion show, each modeling her new outfit. They all looked beautiful! The kids were shocked and cheered for the ladies as they walked through the cafeteria. It was a moment that no one in that lunchroom, including those who worked on the segment, would ever forget: a celebration of all of the hard work these women do for the kids.

That moment went way beyond fashion. It was about appreciation and gratitude for the women who usually stay in the background of our lives. Although these women were used to working as a team, they shined individually in that moment. Normally, their daily outfits were the same, bland, unfashionable, body-draping uniform. Now they were wearing shapely styles, textured fabrics, gorgeous colors, and accessories that would never appear in their work wardrobes. Each outfit was unique and the students were amazed. It was a heartwarming reminder that fashion can help brighten someone's day and bring out buried confidence in the most unexpected places and times.

Watching the segment when it aired was even more thrilling, because it pulled together the whole story. When working on a television show like this, I'm working on different aspects of the segments like pieces of a puzzle, but I don't get to see the results until the end. I was able to watch with the rest of the viewers and kind of forget for a moment that I was the orchestrator. The before-and-afters were significant and exciting. It made me appreciate the real significance a makeover on the outside can bring to the lives of unsuspecting, well-deserving women. A beauty and fashion makeover will never again be quite the same for me.

5.

DRESSING FOR YOUR DATING APP PROFILE

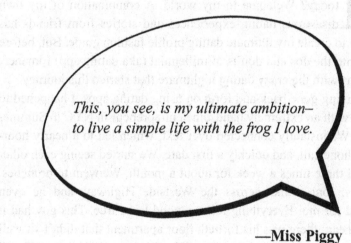

This, you see, is my ultimate ambition—
to live a simple life with the frog I love.

—Miss Piggy

5.

**DRESSING FOR YOUR
DATING APP PROFILE**

Have you ever felt like relationships are nearly impossible today? Welcome to my world. A combination of my own disastrous dating experiences and stories from friends has led me to create my ultimate dating profile fashion guide. But, before I get into the dos and don'ts of millennial (aka dating app) romance, I'll start with the crazy dating nightmare that started this journey.

Having gone back and forth on using dating apps, I happened to match with an extremely handsome entrepreneur in NYC in Summer 2019. We instantly connected over text, which led to a nearly hour-long phone call, and quickly a first date. We started seeing each other around three times a week for about a month. We went to brunches, dinners, long walks across the Westside Highway, and he even cooked for me! Everything felt too good to be true. This guy had it all. I mean, there was his fortieth floor apartment that didn't sit well with me since I hate heights. But OK, if that was his biggest "flaw," I was in.

Right before Thanksgiving I was hosting the Central Park Conservancy after-party, a young adult's fundraiser for Central Park. When I lightly mentioned it to Mr. Too Good to Be True, he told me that he was going to be in Arizona with his family, so I didn't think to invite him as my date considering our relationship was so new. A few days later, he told me he was upset I didn't ask him to change his plans—but we all know that guys don't like "needy" girls, and that would have been full-on needy, no?? I figured I would just bring a friend.

Since I felt bad, I invited him to be my date to a different event that I typically would have attended solo since it was for work. It was a launch event for a new chic car rental company hosted by actress Drew Barrymore. He was excited and I sent him the invite: cocktail attire. He had a few days to get ready. He said he was in.

Is the suspense killing you yet?

The night before the event, Mr. Too Good to Be True confirmed he was going and was super excited. The day of the event, I didn't hear from him in the morning as I usually did. Two hours to go, as I was getting ready, he called me to say he had nothing to wear. I started laughing, thinking he was joking. I asked if he was pretending to be me. But he seriously claimed he didn't have any dress pants, his one button down shirt was wrinkled in the wash, and he'd gotten rid of his "nice" clothes. I was actually SHOCKED. I expected these sorts of calls from my girlfriends before their own date nights, but how did a grown man who was nearly forty not have a pair of PANTS to wear? I reminded him that we live in New York City and there are thousands of stores he could run and find something in, unless he was just using it as an excuse not to go. He said he would go and try but that his body shape was "weird" and it was hard for him to shop. That's when I knew something was going on. Weird body? He was perfectly fit.

An hour later he called me back to say he couldn't find anything. What was I supposed to do? I simply said OK and that I had to go. I was actually really disappointed. I tried to bring someone into my world and open up, but I ended up solo as usual for this special event.

Ultimately, we didn't end up together—CLEARLY!—and it was all because HE didn't have anything to wear (not to mention the truly crazy text messages he sent me after this whole debacle). The very thing that my life revolved around—clothes—was the demise of my short-lived relationship. Nuts, right?

If there's anything that makes me anxious, it's dating. Can't you see why?! Sure, it can be stressful to feel like you have nothing in your closet to wear. Sure, it can be frustrating when you're having a bad day at work and consequently start rethinking your career path; and sure, it can be anxiety provoking when you're working out so hard but aren't seeing results as quickly as you want. But all of these scenarios are ultimately in your control to produce the outcome you want. I personally find dating to be totally out of my control. I see this happening to my friends as well: regardless of gender identification or partner preferences, it is a constant struggle across the board.

My romantic life has been . . . well, interesting, to say the least. As a born and bred New Yorker, the dating culture has always been challenging. After all, this is a city where people are almost entirely focused on their careers. Many who do find their special someone don't feel pressured to settle down until much later than friends in rural communities.

The pool of single women in NYC is huge: gorgeous, bright, successful, and fashionable women, so men don't feel like they have to—or, frankly, want to—commit. The options are unlimited, and men have no "biological clock" that you often hear thrown around to describe women. On top of this, there's the ability to meet someone twenty-four hours a day on an app with a simple swipe.

You don't even have to be set up or go to a bar after work. You just need to go on your phone, download some apps, and there you have it. Endless options right at your fingertips.

My friends and I meet men in a variety of ways, some IRL (in real life) and others on the apps. I actually met my first "significant other" on the train returning to college from NYC to DC after spring break. He was a renowned chef at a very successful restaurant chain. At that point, seeing someone consistently (even though it was short-lived), along with texting and feeling that he cared, was a great boost to my morale. Obviously, it's not enough now, but in that moment, it was, and I was smitten.

Later on, my career took me to parties in cities outside of NYC with big names and interesting faces. Soon, I was meeting guys left and right. I met someone on an airplane from Vegas to NYC. Sadly, there was a shooting next to the runway, so we were on lockdown on the plane for hours. Conversation struck, and we hit it off. That's one way of bridging a connection. We saw each other for a bit.

In that lockdown moment, I realized that you have to look great even when exhausted after work or traveling. You really never know when that special person will appear. Unfortunately, my face was blown up from an infected wisdom tooth that would be removed the next morning. Such is life. Luckily, he didn't seem to mind.

So, how do we deal with modern-day app/cupid experiences? Clearly, it's a bit superficial since our first connection is visual, which means it's even more important than ever to carefully select how we will look in our photos. Ultimately, apps have changed how we date and force us to create a curated presentation of how we want to be seen. I learned the hard way (see: chic car company event dating nightmare) that presentation isn't always accurate or real.

To refresh, I'll break down some of the most popular apps for you to help give you insight on how to curate your profile for each one.

Tinder (launched in 2012): The OG dating app allows users to swipe right to like or swipe left to dislike other users, pairing people together when both swipe right. Among my friends, we label this as the go-to app if you're truly looking for a hook-up and nothing more.

Hinge (2012): My friends tend to have the greatest success on this app. Hinge brands itself as the dating app "designed to be deleted." It uses connections to Facebook friends to facilitate connections, which is appealing to many because matches feel more familiar than other apps.

Bumble (2014): In heterosexual matches, female users make the first contact with the matched male users. In same-sex matches, either person can send a message first. Whitney Wolfe founded Bumble shortly after she left Tinder, which she co-founded. Wolfe describes Bumble as a "feminist dating app." Not every woman feels comfortable initiating on Bumble—I know many of my girlfriends feel this way. However, I actually like that about the app, because I like being in control. As of September 2019, the app had a monthly user base of five million and counting. It's recognized as the second-most popular dating app in the United States after Tinder. In my case, this app has led to longer term relationships. More on this later.

Raya (2015): The "Holy Grail" of dating apps targeted to celebs, influencers, and personalities. Members of this app are usually in the entertainment or arts industries and membership starts at eight dollars per month. Users must be referred by an existing member and then their application is voted on by a membership committee. The acceptance rate for Raya membership applications is approximately eight percent. Profiles are reminiscent of a mini reality TV show. You pick a song as the soundtrack to your slideshow of pictures. There literally isn't one unattractive person on there. I saw Matthew Perry on it once. Just saying.

The League (2015): Another members-only swiping app aimed at professionals. Users connect their LinkedIn and Facebook profiles and then select their criteria for matches. It shows users only five potential matches per day, limiting the pool of options, which to some people can be overwhelming on other apps. Its most popular feature is the twice-a-week "League Live," three 3-minute video dates that the app selects for you. This became especially popular during the start of the coronavirus quarantine, and I predict will change how we date in the future. That is, if we can virtually meet someone before meeting IRL (in real life), it will eliminate wasted time—and honestly, money—with someone who you don't have a connection with.

Of course, there are others, but these apps are most often discussed among my friends.

With all of this said, once you pick your preferred dating app (or apps), the next most important thing is how you portray yourself on your profile. This can easily affect who you end up matching with. Pictures are what everyone is shamelessly basing their attraction off of, which therefore determines whether or not someone is going to swipe "left" or "right" for you and vice versa. The outfits you choose to wear in your photos are also super important. What message are you trying to send? Fun and flirty with crop tops and bikini pics? Reserved and serious with a power suit?

Here are my top eighteen tips for dressing for your dating profile pics—and whether we like it or not, it's the time to show off your sexy side (within your comfort zone, of course):

1. Show yourself in a variety of looks: daytime or work wear, workout or active wear, night out, weekend or laid back.
2. Each outfit should represent a different side of your personality and highlight your interests: if you're a foodie, show yourself eating a great bowl of pasta; if you're a music junkie, rocking out at a concert.
3. Incorporate color without going too bold. Refrain from wearing all black—you want to look open, not closed off!
4. Post both cropped (waist up) and full-length photos.
5. Post at least one photo in a more tight-fitting body-con outfit.
6. Don't be afraid to show a little skin with a crop top or even a bikini pic if you're comfortable doing so.
7. No mirror selfies!!!!
8. If you're someone who likes to be out and about, show a night-out look. Make your potential match dream of what it would be like to take you out on a date!
9. Workout pics should be tasteful, exposing your interests and not just showing how hot you know you look. Think confident, not cocky.
10. No pictures with men—no brothers, dads, or friends. Mixed signals. Avoid at all costs.
11. Don't show off designer clothing labels. It's unattractive.
12. Refrain from oversized jewelry or clunky accessories.
13. Every guy likes a girl in jeans—post a denim pic!
14. If you're into traveling, show off a pic of you at your favorite destination. Adventure seekers will be attracted!
15. No deep V-necks. It's more suggestive than tasteful.
16. Good lighting is key! Avoid the Facetune photo-shopping app (or anything similar). You want to look like yourself!
17. Smile!

18. Be yourself! This is cliché but it's true. If you aren't authentic, you'll match with someone who isn't right for you. Being upfront in your profile is the key to a lasting relationship with someone who's compatible!

It's so important, above all, that you actually *look* like the person in your photos, so don't go and change your image completely. If you are Boho (Bohemian) in the photograph, stay that way. If you are simple and sophisticated, maintain that look.

If you have no idea what to wear, I recommend a few safe bets. I love a skinny high waisted jean with a tucked in bodysuit, a classic pump and little leather or suede jacket. This is great for colder months. For hotter temps, don't be afraid to show a little skin. I love a good sleeveless jumpsuit with a strappy sandal and hoop earring.

My belief: Refrain from overdoing it with the outfit. Instead, let the outfit reflect your style and taste while complementing your inner beauty. A great ensemble + being yourself is just the right combination. Be consistent and have fun looking for your significant other!

6.

PURGE YOUR CLOSET

> *What you wear is how you present yourself to the world, especially today, when human contacts are so quick. Fashion is instant language.*
>
> —**Miuccia Prada**

It was the week leading up to Christmas 2019, and every night was packed with holiday parties. Between brands, television shows, friends, and family hosting events almost every night of December, it felt like New York Fashion Week. I mean this in the sense that I needed a special outfit to wear each and every night, which required thought, time, and product to style.

On the last day of my holiday party circuit, I felt tapped out, like I had absolutely nothing to wear! A dreaded feeling for all women, I'm sure. I had already worn all of my fun, colorful sparkly holiday-esque pieces. I had a cute little black dress that hadn't made its way out of my closet yet, but it just didn't feel festive enough for where I was going: first to my dad's office holiday party, then to a holiday party for a cool brand downtown in Soho, and finally to a dessert date with a guy I had met at Art Basel, an art fair, in Miami a few weeks before (this was literally the only hour we could both meet up in a month).

Just a few hours before it was time to get going, I came to terms with the fact that I *really* didn't have anything to wear and needed to go buy something new. I *hate* going shopping at the last minute, especially when I'm on the hunt for something specific. I can feel the fashion pressure brewing! I usually buy my clothes as I find them at leisure, and then I coordinate/style them based on where I'm going.

But not this time. I mad-dashed to Zara, thinking I could find something cute and affordable, but it was a hardcore fail. It was like the entire holiday collection was gone. There was nothing! Bloomingdales was just across the street, so I ran there to find Dakota, my friend who works at the store. We went through racks and racks of dresses and skirts, and it was definitely challenging to find something sparkly and shiny—much more so than I thought. Eventually, I found the perfect little mini black long sleeve cinched-waist dress embellished with gold, hot pink, and green mini sequins. I belted it with a vintage Gucci belt that was handed down to me by my grandma, and I added black tights, booties, and a clutch to pull it all together. Finally, I was ready to go!

The "I have nothing to wear" dilemma is definitely the most common complaint I hear from women on TV, in my DMs, and in person. I'm sure many of you can relate! The worst is when we don't take the time to "shop" our own closets, whether it's for a date or a girl's night out in NYC, and instead immediately purchase something new. Bad habit, I know. But I'm just as guilty as you are, and in some cases, as proven above, you give in.

There's something about the "new" that makes what's currently in my closet feel, well, wrong. Even though I spent just as much time purchasing those "older" items as I did the new, they just don't look as fresh, on-trend, or as flattering as they did when I originally bought them. My body is constantly changing too, which requires constant wardrobe adjustments.

I *want* to wear something new and current each day, but frankly this is impractical, and it becomes extremely expensive. It's just not reality. Luckily, many brands I work with generously send me their new items, which helps underwrite my obsession with new clothes. But again, this has become a bad fashion habit.

This "nothing to wear" problem has a simple solution: closet organization. Sure, simply organizing your clothes won't magically make new ones appear, but this is where it all begins. If having "nothing to wear" is the most common fashion dilemma I hear, then closet organization comes in close second. And they are more related than you'd think!

Through over twenty-six years of being clothing-obsessed, I've learned how to make my wardrobe a priority and take control of my closet—keeping it meticulously arranged for everyday ease. This is particularly critical when living in NYC. Closet space is limited and even if you want to keep everything you have ever purchased, it's impossible. Remember Carrie Bradshaw's original closet in *Sex and the City*, pre-Mr. Big? That's the norm.

On that note, many fellow fashionistas buy rolling racks and park them in their bedrooms and living rooms like a piece of furniture. You can see this on your favorite fashion influencers' Instagram accounts. I'm also guilty of this. It works until you have a date over, and they realize that these metal racks take over your apartment (and life). A little TMI for most guys. If he's the one, he'll hopefully get over it and develop a little fashion obsession too.

Each season, my secret to success is that I try to purge what I don't wear. It is difficult to give up a favorite outfit, but sometimes it is too worn to continue wearing, and I need more closet space! I also purge items that look awkward (unless the fashion cycle brings them back!), including anything that is feather trimmed, neon, western, etc. I recommend affordable stores like Zara or H&M for trendier pieces—you won't be upset if you don't wear it after a season because it did not break the bank. A few outfits have great karma: You got that job, you were asked on a second date, and so on. But if I haven't worn something for a season or it's no longer bringing me joy, then it's time for it to go, Marie Kondo style.

Every item of clothing that you choose to wear should always bring out your best self. If you own something that you don't associate with positivity, it's simply not worth having around. I got rid of the cropped leather jacket from Topshop that I was wearing when I broke up with my first "serious" flame. We closed a chapter together, so I said goodbye to that outfit. When we look our best, most times we end up *feeling* our best too, and it's easier for us to achieve our goals and do what makes us happy.

Recently, I received an email from a company that organizes closets for a hundred dollars an hour, with a thirty-hour discount! That's three thousand dollars! If I had three thousand dollars to spend, I would much rather purchase contents to fill my closet than pay someone to organize it. A Chanel bag is sounding good!

Therefore, I am my own closet organizer, with the help of my mom who is an expert. She started her career in retail, where she organized sales floors at department stores. She learned the best ways to display by style, color, and patterns. It's a science, for sure, and her methods really work. So take a few hours on a Sunday afternoon or whenever you can squeeze in some downtime, because it will change your "getting ready" process like no other. Believe me, it is worth the effort. And since moms really do know best, let's look to mine for her best tips and tricks.

MY MOM'S CLOSET PURGE

Step 1: Break It Up. Divide your wardrobe into categories: work clothes, weekend clothes, and dressy outfits are my three go-tos. Then divide each category by pieces: blouses, tanks, pants, jeans, etc. You can even break it down further. Searching for a pair of jeans? Group them together to decide which one fits the occasion. Create your own little boutique of options: skinny, mom jeans, high-waisted, bell bottoms, and so on.

Step 2: Color Code It. I've found it best to organize by color first, and then by sleeve length: sleeveless, short-sleeve, and long-sleeve. Follow my rainbow guide for color: white, cream, yellow, orange, pink, red, blue, purple, green, brown, grey, and then black. Patterned clothing should have its own area and be organized by the predominant color. Coordinate slacks by color and then the short cropped to the longer pants. Arrange dresses by rainbow color and then by sleeve length. You will be amazed at how professional this looks, and you can quickly "shop your wardrobe" for fashionable styles.

Step 3: Seasons of Clothes. If you have a second closet in your home, put out-of-season clothing away until you need it (if you don't have a second closet, make use of the extra space under your bed or purchase an extra rack). If it's wintertime and you have an upcoming warm weather vacation, you'll know you can find those items quickly.

Step 4: Feet First. Accessories are especially challenging due to space. Shoes tend to be the most difficult. I purchase sliding plastic boxes at the Container Store and stack up the shoes, so that I can see what is in them. I have so many shoes that I often feel like I'm literally living in these boxes, but such is a fashion girl's dilemma. My favorite shoe trick: Paste a photo on each shoebox so you can easily see the pair without opening the box. A little more work, but manageable and it saves you time in the long-run.

Step 5: Bag Lady. Accessories like purses are best placed on shelves if you have them available. They also make for chic décor if you're ready to expose your belongings—I do this. My bookshelves substitute as display cases for my purses; I have not regretted this decision one bit.

Step 6: Shiny Things. Jewelry is good in drawers or on top of the dresser, again in divided plastic boxes that the Container Store has in every shape and size. The best advice is to have everything visible, so you can quickly select the best choices. You'll be shocked at what you find—like little treasures when you've forgotten about them for so long.

Step 7: Purging. Now the question is what to do with the pile of items you never wear. If you keep your clothes clean and looking great, then you will find lots of opportunities to either donate or resell your clothes. There are great online and retail destinations like the RealReal. They will come to your home to pick up your items, or you can mail directly to them depending on where you live. It is exciting to receive surprise checks for your old clothes, which you can use for new purchases. Think of this as your modern-day piggy bank. If the clothing is too worn or is a brand resellers don't take, deliver them to your local Good Will, and they will provide you with a tax deduction form. It feels great to donate to a good cause. I'm always amazed at how crowded these places are with people looking for great bargains. Remember, your old item may be someone else's new found gem.

One last tip: I have wasted far too much time closet hunting for a particular black t-shirt, a tight-fitting bodycon dress, or favorite jeans, but could not find them. Yet this rarely happens to me today. Now I prepare my outfits the night before, all styled, so that I can focus on my hair and makeup and not on my clothing choices the following morning.

People say you want to live in a happy space, but ultimately, you also want to *get dressed* in a happy space. Getting dressed is likely one of the first things you do every morning, and doing so without havoc—being able to go into your closet, know where everything is, and not feel overwhelmed—will help serve as the foundation to having a successful and accomplished day. Sure, you'll still have moments like my Holiday Party 2019 panic-shop, but it won't happen nearly as often if you keep your clothes and accessories organized and up-to-date.

7.

MASTERING TRENDS
AT ANY AGE

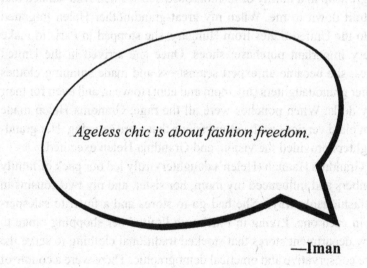

Ageless chic is about fashion freedom.

—Iman

I grew up in a family of fashion-obsessed women who handed that trait down to me. When my great-grandmother Helen migrated to the United States from Hungary, she stopped in Paris to make a very important purchase: shoes. Once she arrived in the United States, she became an expert seamstress and made stunning clothes for her granddaughters (my mom and aunt) to wear, and even for their baby dolls. When ponchos were all the rage, Grandma Helen made them plaid versions with yellow fringe that were amazing. Her granddaughters provided the vision, and Grandma Helen executed.

Grandma Hannah (Helen's daughter) truly led our pack of family members and influenced my mom, her sister, and my two cousins in her fashionable ways. She had go-to stores and a favorite salesperson in each one. Living in Pittsburgh limited her shopping range to a few department stores that stocked traditional clothing to serve the more conservative and practical demographic. There were a couple of small boutiques, but for the most part, the latest fashion trends were nearly impossible to find.

Before the days of online shopping, there was mail order, but that took forever. Grandma Hannah used to make annual shopping trips to New York City each August to get her hands on the latest fall fashions. Additionally, she and my grandfather Marvin went to

Europe each year, and Paris was first for Grandma's wardrobe. For good measure, they also went to London so Grandpa could update his wardrobe. My grandpa wasn't a fashion expert, but he loved fine clothes and Grandma coordinated his outfits each and every day.

Throughout the year when she wasn't making the trips, stores would send her clothing on memo; meaning that she didn't have to pay for anything in advance (like Stitch Fix or Trunk Club today). In her case they didn't even ask for her credit card because there was a mutual trust. Grandma Hannah was comfortable knowing that the sales associates knew her style and could select items she would love. Simultaneously, the stores trusted that my grandmother would either purchase the items or if they didn't fit she would expertly rewrap, package, and ship the clothes back as soon as possible. This went on for decades. Grandma Hannah's style was defined, classic, and sophisticated. She was not afraid to experiment with color or patterns. Silhouettes were sleek and refined, never showing too much skin, but also consistent with the times. She carefully planned her outfits every night, which, as you learned in the previous chapter, is an essential part of my nightly routine as well. Always confident, she glimmered in her outfits, attracting stares when she walked in a room, whether at a party or the hair salon. To this day, friends and family recall that she was always perfectly dressed. It was fun to watch, and something I aspired to emulate.

My mom's sister lives in Chicago, and me, my mom, and my aunt speak by phone almost daily. Fashion is our favorite topic: a new purchase, a new designer collection, or a new store in our respective cities. Fashion is in our blood and definitely keeps us connected. Clothing really is more symbiotic than many might think.

My mom and aunt frequently stress that they should avoid fashion brands their children—my cousins and I—wear because they feel it's too young for them. If we're wearing it, they shouldn't be, so they're always searching for an age appropriate version of the trend.

How can women across generations adapt younger trends, while also remaining comfortable and stylish? *Harper's Bazaar*, one of my favorite fashion magazines, makes wardrobe recommendations for every generation of women, ranging from those in their twenties to their seventies. I brought this concept to life in my debut segment for the *Today Show* with *Hoda & Jenna*. Using four real families and three generations of women, I showed how every generation can master the same fashion trend (more on this later!).

While many believe that there are no rules when it comes to fashion—and I agree to a certain extent—you can apply useful guidelines. My suggested guidelines fall into three categories: style, color (including solids, prints, patterns), and fit.

STYLE

The "style" part is tricky because it depends on your own take on fashion and has little to do with what's trending in retail, in the media, and on social media. Yes, you can remain true to yourself while incorporating popular trends into your wardrobe.

Think of the Patricia Fields, Diane Keatons, Anna Wintours, and Iris Apfels of the world, to name a few. They created their own unique style and no matter which trend is "in" or "out," they wear what they want and look great. Patricia is known for her bold use of colors and patterns; Diane for her signature turtlenecks; Anna for her larger-than-life sunglasses; and Iris for her chunky jewelry. They've each cultivated an exterior version of themselves for which we remember and think of them. This is essentially an instinct that you develop over time, and one I truly believe comes with age. The more comfortable you are in your own skin, the more comfortable you will feel with your clothing choices. They're intertwined.

For me personally, my style fully developed after graduating college. After a certain number of years, you realize what works and what doesn't, what you want to experiment with, and what you want to steer clear from. If you're still searching for your personal style, I suggest making a list of everything you like and don't like. From trends to fit to silhouettes to fabrics—you name it. In many cases, the process of elimination can actually help lead you to your answer. You can also look at other people's style that you like and then combine the inspiration you've gotten from them with your list of what you do like.

It's perfectly OK for your style to evolve—after all, style is not finite. Fashion, on the other hand, is finite, because we're always going to see new trends and new products. That won't change. But with different phases of life comes different ways you like to express yourself, therefore creating a style evolution. Certainly there are style principles that don't change, so when you look back years from now there's some sort of consistency and understanding of why you made those fashion choices.

COLOR

Gen-Z and Gen-X typically opt for brighter, bolder hues. It's a way to make a statement. Younger shoppers can get away with taking color risks, many opting for monochromatic outfits (wearing one color from head to toe) and wearing louder hues (think neon) to settings as casual as the gym, or as fancy as a gala. Women of my mom's generation—fifty plus—tend to prefer darker tones as their base, while incorporating pops of color, creating a more classic combination/aesthetic. A huge color story trend that made a splash in recent years (2012) is millennial pink. It's a trend that literally refuses to go away! It's mutated to include shades from beige to Barbie pink to a peachy-salmon combo, and beyond. While some might assume it's meant to be girly, it's truly become androgynous and no longer is just associated with the girly wardrobes in movies like *Clueless* and *Mean Girls*. It's become more than just a color but a way of being relevant in fashion and beyond.

PATTERNS

A fun way to carve out your style, indeed, is with patterns. Popular prints over the years have included florals, 1920s art deco graphics, punchy '70s-inspired combos, plaid, stripes, polka dots, and more. For those who are just trying to define their style, incorporate these patterns in small doses with a t-shirt, or even an accessory like a clutch or shoe. A bold print might not be for everyone, but it's a fun way to be adventurous. Worse comes to worst, you try it out, decide it's not for you, and continue on your fashion scavenger hunt to finding what's best for you. Animal prints are a print we see year after year: leopard, cheetah, snakeskin, you name it. This is a great starting point because many of these animal prints come in neutral colors, which might be the most comfortable place for you to start. If you're ready to take a fashion risk, experiment with mixing patterns. I love wearing a polka dot blouse with a striped pant. This sort of risk is a great way to really own your look. It's a way to really differentiate yourself, because it's not every day you'll see someone rocking this aesthetic.

FIT

The worst thing you can do is wear clothing that doesn't fit. I don't care how much or how little you spend on an outfit. Wearing clothes that are too baggy, tight, long, or too short is fashion sabotage. Don't fall into a trap of purchasing something you love but which doesn't look good on you. It must be flattering. If I even have a little doubt when trying on a piece of clothing, I usually FaceTime my mom for her opinion, and then we typically come to the conclusion that it's not worth the purchase. It never hurts to get a second opinion, but you probably already know in your gut it's not right.

A lot of women tend to buy the wrong size of clothing for multiple reasons. One, if you're shopping online, it can be hard to determine how the clothes run. Each website typically provides a size guide, but I always suggest buying multiple sizes of each item so you can try, and then return what doesn't work. Today many brands like Lululemon offer a virtual FaceTime appointment with a sales associate to guide you through the selection and sizing process. I also find many women actually buy clothing that's too big for them because they see themselves as bigger than they really are. I always tell my mom she buys tops that are at least two sizes too big. She definitely doesn't have body issues but when we're looking at ourselves in the mirror every day, it's easy to develop an outlook that may or may not be what is actually reality.

In contrast, I also had a girlfriend who struggled with weight loss growing up. She always bought clothing at least two sizes too small because she said she was going to use them as an incentive to lose weight and then be able to wear them. I never understood this but we each have our own ways of thinking.

I have some tips to combat body image issues when finding your style. First, dress for how you look and the size you really are in the moment of making your purchases. Second, don't be embarrassed by the size—what's most embarrassing is wearing something that doesn't fit. My tailor once told me that when you're buying or fitting pants, you should be able to fit a few fingers inside the waistline. That way, on days you're feeling bloated, you have some room— this is especially helpful during "time of the month" days. Third, always steer clear from pants with pockets (this excludes jeans). I find it always makes me look wider than I actually am. Lastly, when it comes to blazers or leather jackets, make sure you can hug someone in it. If you can't, it means it's too tight around your chest area and it'll potentially look like you're wearing someone else's clothing.

Also realize that not every item of clothing looks great on all women. For example, I can't wear button down shirts. I'm heavier chested and there is not a shirt that doesn't have a button that pops off when I put one on. It's critical to spend time at a variety of stores, find what silhouettes look the best, and also determine which sizes of each brand fits best on you. For example, it's hard for me to wear J.Crew as an XS looks more like a large on me. It just depends on your body and finding your perfect match.

Since I've lost my cupcake-weight from college and incorporated exercise into my life to keep my body and mind healthy and regulate my mood, my confidence definitely increased dramatically. I started wearing bodycon clothing that sometimes honestly would even be a bit provocative—not to show anything off to anyone else but because it made me feel better. While I've had fun dressing like this in my twenties, this isn't something I can see myself doing later in life when I'm [hopefully] married in my thirties and having children. It just doesn't seem appropriate (to me). So whether a short skirt, a low-cut shirt, or a tight pair of pants, it all comes down to the "right" look for where you are in life. If you're in your fifties or above, a great option is a sexy pant with slits on the side. You can also try a long sleeve off the shoulder top, which shows a little bit of skin but not too much. It's all about balance.

As mentioned, my debut segment on *Hoda & Jenna* (the *Today*

Show) showcased the concept of how women of every generation can master the same fashion trends. I identified three families with three generations of women to style the top three summer fashion trends of 2019—distressed denim, puffed sleeves, and playful plaids—trends likely to remain in vogue well into the future. You can rock these trends at any age. Here's how I broke it down on the show:

DISTRESSED DENIM

You don't have to be young to incorporate distressed denim into your wardrobe. Every generation can fashion different versions of it depending on how much of a statement you're looking to make. While the younger generation tends to go down the "more ripped off the better" path with major rips (you'll see them letting their knees go cold—literally—with major rips around the area), those who are older can opt for a subtle distressed style, with just enough of a worn-out look. It's all about finding what's within your comfort zone.

Millennials/Gen-Z: I dressed the youngest in the family in overalls for a fun way to incorporate distressed denim with a playful silhouette. Overalls are youthful, and can easily be spiced up by layering a fun pattern underneath. On the segment, I used tie dye since it was the trend of the season, but you can always find an inexpensive option to spice up as the times change. You can also go as distressed as you want. I don't particularly like too many rips when it comes to clothing, but it's totally up to you.

Baby Boomers/Gen-X: I love a distressed denim pencil skirt. For the segment, I found a version that hit right at the knee, so the casual fabric looked more refined and flattering. Another tip for moms is to find an option that's high-wasted. This is perfect for women of any body type. Pair it with a bodysuit blouse that can easily be tucked in underneath, and you're good to go!

Matriarchs: If you're the grandmother, you don't necessarily have to make the distressed denim the star of your outfit. It's best to incorporate it through a piece that can easily be taken on and off throughout the day/night. For the segment, I put grandma in a denim jacket, opting for a lighter wash so it looked distressed but didn't feature rips. This trick shows just a *hint* of the trend. We had fun pairing the denim jacket with a party pant (that is, a pant that's in a statement color or pattern).

PUFFED SLEEVES

Puffed sleeves continuously promise to be bigger and bolder every year. They're the perfect combination of feminine-meets-masculine when wanting to wear an outfit that gives off ultimate girl boss vibes. Everyone from Queen Elizabeth to Elizabeth Taylor to today's modern style stars (from the Hadids to the Kardashians) have at some point donned this trend. You can incorporate it via so many similar silhouettes that it works for just about any occasion.

Millennials/Gen-Z: If you're in your twenties, have fun going for a bold puff sleeve jumpsuit in a fresh color that is trending that season. I absolutely love a good jumpsuit—they can make for great day-to-night transition pieces and are super elongating, especially if you're petite like me. They also look great on taller women. This is exactly how I dressed our youngest generation for the *Today Show*.

Baby Boomers/Gen-X: For moms, there's something super chic and effortless about a puff sleeve dress. While a puff sleeve can sometimes look edgy, an easy way to go for a softer version is to opt for a fresh and feminine print.

Matriarchs: Florals are always a safe and classic bet. Your grandma doesn't have to be left out when it comes to the puffed sleeve trend! I find that most women have a staple pair of black pants that are their go-tos. On the show, we spiced it up by incorporating a puff sleeve blouse with it. This enabled our oldest generation to stay within her comfort zone for the bottom portion of her look, while having some fun with the top half. Think of it as a happy medium. No matter how old you are this is certainly a trend that can be worn all year round.

PLAYFUL PLAIDS

Plaid prints are no doubt here to stay. Case in point? Just look at Burberry! The brand has been around for years and years and is still very much relevant in the fashion world. Even better? Plaid can hands down be fashionable for women of any age because there are many different versions of the print.

Millennials/Gen-Z: Gingham is a plaid pattern that is super youthful and fresh, typically seen in the warmer months. Whether you opt for a cropped pant or a high wasted short, it's a happy print that will instantly make you feel like your outfit is spot-on.

Baby Boomers/Gen-X: For the mom on my segment, I dressed her in a slightly bigger plaid—medium checks—in a more dressed-up silhouette. The style of the clothing you select can easily elevate a pattern, especially one that's considered to typically be more casual.

Matriarchs: I love a plaid maxi dress during the summer months. It's super playful yet still sophisticated. For grandmas, try to find a version that's sleeveless and perhaps comes with a belt that can cinch the dress at the waste. This look is perfect for a picnic or daytime party/lunch! On the show, we dressed our oldest generation in a black and white plaid pant with an easy blazer and statement clutch and shoe. Chic, effortless, and can easily be dressed up or down depending on the occasion.

Recently I was in Neiman Marcus in Palm Beach and a sales associate came up to my mom. Not unusual. But then, the associate said she knew Grandma Hannah when she worked at another store on Worth Avenue about thirty years ago. Talk about a good memory! Not only did this associate remember how sweet and kind my grandmother was, but she explained how her sense of fashion and refinement influenced her own fashion. My grandmother was the master of defining her own style and didn't waiver, even with changing trends. This is an important takeaway to spend some time thinking about how you want to look and what you enjoy wearing. You never know who it could impact down the line.

Ultimately, the women in your family can wear the fashion trends they love while remaining appropriate and comfortable for their age. Stripes, sequins, animal prints, neon hues, pastels, sparkles, metallics—the options are endless! It's worth experimenting and I'm sure you will be pleasantly surprised with the results. Just always make sure that the clothes fit you perfectly and you're staying true to your own style. There is nothing that will destroy a gorgeous outfit more quickly than poor fit. So, the next time you, your mom or grandma, or whoever in your family think you all can't wear the same fashion trend, think again!

8.

WHAT JACKIE O AND MEGHAN MARKLE TAUGHT ME

If I can have any impact, I want women to feel good about themselves and have fun with fashion.

—Michelle Obama

W omen often communicate their thoughts and opinions through their clothing choices. Take a classic example like Marilyn Monroe, who dressed provocatively to exude sex appeal. In 1977, *The Women's Dress for Success Book* by John T. Molloy had women dressing "like men" in suits in order to get the job they wanted. Diane Keaton (and her on-screen persona from the same year, Annie Hall) favored neck ties. It was truly a "thing." Thoughts and opinions via clothing choices have only become louder and more pronounced since.

The wives of heads of state typically share their personalities and perspectives based on the designers they select, what they choose to wear, and the accessories they incorporate into their ensembles, even when (historically) uttering only a few words. Speaking through fashion selections can be a powerful statement and can influence generations. In this chapter, I'll dive into some of the most talked-about female political fashion icons in the United States and overseas.

Years ago, I visited my grandmother and was surprised to find a sunglass collection that rivaled mine today. She was a petite woman, like me, but her drawers were filled with huge and oversized sunglasses, many with thick black-rimmed frames. I asked my mom what this was about, and she nonchalantly said it was the "Jackie O" effect.

She was referring to Jaqueline Kennedy Onassis, a bona fide style icon and the wife of twenty-fifth US President John F. Kennedy. (It was rumored that Jackie spent more on her annual wardrobe than her husband's presidential salary). In her elegant, sophisticated, and subtle way, she stole attention from her husband during their many travels. We rarely heard her speak, but her power was clear; she became a major inspiration to women around the world and influenced how many women dressed. Signature accessories included large sunglasses, wide brimmed hats, scarves worn around her head, and gloves and bows. She also wore amazing coats, equestrian styles, and glamorous gowns, often bearing her shoulders.

Like many modern first ladies, Jackie Kennedy was associated with a famous designer of her day: Oleg Cassini. I had not heard of him until last summer, when my mom, an avid collector, said she was bidding on items from Oleg Cassini's estate. She had the winning bid for an amazing collection of his original sketches of clothes he designed for Jackie Kennedy during her White House years.

Jackie Kennedy followed her first lady tenure with a job as a well-respected book editor. Next in notable first lady fashion came actress Nancy Reagan, lawyer Michele Obama, and most recently, fashion model Melania Trump.

Nancy Reagan was a friend and fan of legendary designers Oscar de la Renta, Bill Blass, and Adolfo. She was often seen in show-stopping bright cherry red clothing. While she was criticized for her expensive ensembles laden with diamonds and furs, some of her trends, like matching jackets and skirts and jackets with shoulder pads, were being copied by working women of that era.

Unlike her predecessors, Michelle Obama wasn't criticized for great spending. She was elegant but always looked practical. She was the first to mix high and low brands, which made her style more attainable to women and admired by the press. She wore American icons like Ralph Lauren and Michael Kors but also fashioned new up and coming designers like Narciso Rodriguez, Isabel Toledo, and Jason Wu. She was very influential in putting them on the fashion map. Don't forget MILLY's Michelle Smith, who Obama wore in her national portrait gallery painting, giving Smith a new level of exposure that made her one of the more talked-about designers. Obama also combined designer creations with outside the box accessories, like floral leather broaches and J.Crew separates. Retrospectively, the only controversial thing she perhaps did at that time was bear her shoulders by frequently wearing sleeveless dresses and showing her beautifully toned arms. A little rebellious, perhaps, but showing her independence and her stance as a totally modern woman. Plus, who wouldn't be envious of those arms? I want them!

Fast forward to Melania Trump, who dresses elegantly in famous couture designs. She's known to select her outfits herself, in addition to working with stylist Herve Pierre—the former fashion designer for Carolina Herrera. The media often reports that Melania's outfits carry a hidden message—for example, that the white suit and white hat reminiscent of *Scandal*'s Olivia Pope, the Gucci pussy bow blouse, and the army green jacket stating, "I Really Don't Care, Do U?" conveyed a political statement. If this was the case, then applause to her for using a nonverbal means of communication to tell the world what she's thinking or feeling or that she wants to keep all of us guessing. Whatever her intentions, it worked. However, it certainly isn't unusual for a first lady to dress (like any of us would) for the occasion that we are attending.

In the midst of the above "I Really Don't Care, Do U?" controversy, I received a call from the nationally syndicated show *Inside Edition* that President Trump and the first lady were off for their first state visit to the United Kingdom. They wanted me to educate viewers on the significance of the first lady's outfits that she wore throughout the trip. I stated that she mixed a range of American and international brands, including Burberry and Dolce & Gabbana, to pay homage to the United States and Europe. When I'm off the air, this skill—being able to identify the brands of clothing before it's released—comes in handy. It helps me read people instantly and get a better sense for their style and mood of the day.

Americans have always been mesmerized with Britain's royal family. For many, this obsession began with Princess Diana, who loved fashion and became an icon. Although she died when I was only three years old, I knew that her gorgeous gowns, mini cocktail dresses, and amazing street wear would continue to influence global fashion. Experimenting with lengths, colors, and new trends, Diana's curated style still looks fresh today.

Kate Middleton, Duchess of Cambridge, is always meticulously dressed, yet more formal and traditional. Even her casual clothing is crisp and pulled together. She looks appropriate and professional, if not safe and practical, at all times. This makes sense since her husband Prince William is also more serious in his own role as the second in line to the British throne. Kate's go-to British designers include L.K. Bennet, Alexander McQueen, the fashion brand Reiss, designer Erdem Moralioglu, jewelry designer Monica Vinader, and often the fashion store Zara, which offers attainable styles for women for less.

Finally, American actress turned royal Meghan Markle is perfectly styled, always elegant, and sophisticated. She definitely played it safe as a Royal Family newbie. When she married Prince Harry, her Givenchy gown was understated, and she barely wore makeup. She typically wears solids in deep rich tones and form fitting silhouettes, showing her figure but in an appropriate and conservative manner. Meghan definitely mixes the best of the British and American designers.

Nearly two years into Meghan's role as the Duchess of Sussex, *Inside Edition* called to ask if I could be at the studio as soon as possible. Meghan and Harry had just announced they are leaving the United Kingdom for Canada, and Meghan was seen in a green parka with faux fur that she wore in 2017 and a cable knit sweater that was previously seen on her in 2013 when she appeared in her TV show *Suits*. "Meghan is making a huge shift in her wardrobe, going from royal to everyday mom," I said on the show. "She's trying to show us that she's like every modern woman and it's ok to wear outfits she's been seen in. She doesn't care about being an outfit repeater." Meghan's wardrobe transformation is yet another example of how what we wear on the outside reflects what's going on inside.

Naturally, our obsession with both American first ladies and British royalty will endure for years to come, and we will continue to wonder what their clothing choices communicate to the world. But most importantly, the fashion choices of these influential women and others from decades past through today show how our individual fashion choices can be used like a voice. Fashion helps us make statements, voice opinions, and be creative in ways words sometimes can't.

9.

TIPPING THE SCALE

Everyone is shocked by things that are different . . . but it will be normal one day to see every size on the runway.

—**Christian Siriano**

When I was growing up, I never thought about my weight. My mom cooked almost every night, so what I ate was essentially chosen for me. I loved sweets, (and still do) and I always had a healthy relationship with food. Unlike many of the girls around me, I didn't control the food I ate or not eat something that I really wanted. I never overanalyzed how I looked in clothes and kind of accepted myself as is. I was happy with how I looked, and confident with my outfit choices. I was fortunate to have a caring family that enabled me to develop this healthy relationship to body image.

However, since I went to an all-girls school until college, I was surrounded by friends who sometimes grew up with different circumstances and constantly, obsessively discussed body image. The frequent complaints were: "My hips are too wide!" "My stomach isn't flat enough!" "My thighs don't have a gap!" The list went on and on. Remember that iconic scene in *Mean Girls* when Gretchen Weiner says, "My hairline is so weird" and the rest of the clique follows suit with "My pores are huge" and "My nail beds suck"? Honestly, the rants became background noise to me, because at that time I couldn't relate. But these insecurities, retrospectively, represented something bigger. Your weight, health, and exercise habits can impact all aspects of your life, including how you dress. Feeling good impacts looking good and creating this foundation early is advised.

My petite figure continued through high school and I simply took it for granted. I was required to take physical education through my senior year—essentially light exercise—and I enjoyed taking spin classes at Soul Cycle, but it wasn't routine and far from an obsession. It was more of a social activity with a few of my girlfriends. We loved the music and the hot instructors (ugh, Denis—the instructor with the hair of all hair; he looked like the modern-day Fabio!), but the most we'd go was twice a month.

Then, when I was eighteen, I entered my freshman year of college at George Washington University in Washington, D.C., and there was a *lot* of talk about the "freshman fifteen" (a typical weight gain of fifteen pounds). Even then, I didn't take this phenomenon seriously; it applied to others and not me. I felt totally immune to it, concluding that the freshman fifteen was linked to horrific eating habits like late night pizza (everyone in D.C. went to Jumbo Slice, the after-party hot spot also known as the hub for the best pizza in town) and drinking lots of alcohol (a prerequisite for Jumbo Slice).

College drinking is such a major contributing factor to weight gain and luckily it wasn't my thing. I've never been fond of alcohol, never experimented with it in high school, and didn't even drink until I turned twenty-one in college. I still don't drink *that* much to this day. Yet little did I know, the freshman fifteen had its own special trigger in my life: cupcakes. Give me some Red Velvet and *Sex and the City* reruns and I was good.

During my first week of college I met two boys who grew up in Pittsburgh, my mom's hometown. They all went to the same high school. We quickly realized that we all were focused on our work and careers and *hated* drinking and going to clubs. So much for fun college times! So, when my girlfriends went out to the bars and clubs, the three of us tried different restaurants around D.C.—pizza places, Chinese, Italian, the list continues. Retrospectively, I was ordering more than I realized to keep up with the boys' larger appetites. Even when I started with healthy salad, I had French fries on the side. Pasta alone apparently wasn't enough, so I added bread. Lots of it.

To top it off, dessert became a habit each and every night. I am not talking about shared desserts with my friends or a few bites of a chocolate cake. Let me get real with you: think mile high cakes, bread puddings, cookies, and pies. There was no stopping me at Old Ebbitt Grill, a restaurant next to the White House known for top politicians meeting and negotiating policies. For me, this is where I negotiated (with myself) how much dessert I could eat in one night. D.C. was also a launching pad for several amazing cupcake emporiums, and I suddenly became a cupcake aficionado! Loads and loads of cupcakes in every flavor combination imaginable from s'mores to banana.

Cupcakes became my freshman year guilty pleasure and I downed them as frequently as my friends downed cans of beer. I became a regular at all the hot spots: Georgetown Cupcake, Sprinkles, and Baked and Wired, to name a few. When popular television shows like *DC Cupcakes* featured my favorite cupcake emporiums, I felt even more justified in my sugar addiction.

I remember the very day I realized I'd gained weight. I had just finished rushing for my sorority. I put on a black dress for a girl's night out and my stomach was truly bulging out of it. It was a "food baby" on steroids. I couldn't believe it. It's even hard writing about this now, years later, because it was such a raw moment. I totally lost control. At first I thought I was just bloated (maybe my period was coming?), but I was actually "bloated" for the prior three weeks. Looking at myself in the mirror, I was beyond upset, so I decided to go weigh myself on a scale. I'd gained thirty pounds. I'm really petite (five foot one) so a thirty-pound weight gain on someone with my height and build was impossible to hide and I didn't handle it well. I became the latest person to embark on a trend that I had not been planning on following: not just the freshman fifteen, but the freshman thirty. I was devastated, to say the least.

My heart was racing, and I started crying—for days. I just couldn't believe that I let myself go and didn't recognize that I was gaining excessive weight as I was literally eating my way through the nation's capital. What had I done? In the moment, I didn't realize how much I was eating or that *what* I was eating was actually impacting how I looked. I was blind, like Shallow Hal—the 2001 movie starring Jack Black and Gwyneth Paltrow. I loved watching that movie as a kid, but even today it's hard to watch because it reminds me of my freshman thirty experience. Looking into my distorted college dorm room mirror, I saw a huge version of myself staring back; not only was my stomach bigger, but my face was too. Now when I look back at pictures of myself on Facebook, I can see the cupcake phase of my life written all over me.

Weeks went by and I still felt horrible, so I called my grandpa Marvin because he was the only person who could make what felt like the worst scenario seem OK. He told me I'm beautiful and I would deal with it like I do with everything else. That was helpful, but it would take a long time for me to feel confident in my own body again.

Trying to put clothes on that I'd bought at the start of school was probably the most difficult part of this whole experience. I couldn't fit in my jeans, my tops were tight, and wearing a dress seemed like an impossible task that I couldn't even fathom. I was only comfortable in stretchy leggings and sweatshirts. My friends used to compare me to Lady Gaga. Now I felt like I was twice her size—not literally, but that's how I felt. I couldn't even wear my favorite clothes anymore. My confidence faded quickly. There was no way I was going to feel good walking around in my little miniskirts or tight dresses. I thought: *Who would want to see me like THIS?*

Returning home for Thanksgiving during my freshman year, I met my girlfriend Clio for lunch. The shocked look on her face made me really uncomfortable. We went shopping at a store across the street from the restaurant and shared a dressing room to try on some clothes. Her shock escalated, and she couldn't stop staring at my larger body.

I knew exactly what she was thinking and was horrified. I asked her, "Do I really look that terrible?!"

She said, "No! You just . . . changed." Translation: I was fat. Clio was trying to be kind, but she further confirmed my deepest fears.

My college years from then on out fully revolved around my weight. It was all I talked about. I became like the girls I'd grown up with. I complained about every inch of my body. I took pictures of myself, comparing how I looked every month. I was obsessed, over analyzing everything. I hired a New York trainer to help me work out when I came home on weekends and all school breaks and vacations. I decided to try out a diet since nothing else seemed to be helping, reducing as many fatty foods as possible, but I didn't see a significant change. I went to Soul Cycle in addition to my trainer, which only made my legs feel larger and my body bulkier. Like so many women, I felt lost and stuck in this big trap of diet and exercise that I didn't know how to get out of.

Three years later, as a senior in college, I was even more focused on how much food I was eating daily. I was also more diligent with an exercise routine, yet I still only lost five pounds of my cupcake weight. Losing weight is ROUGH! It's no easy task, and everyone loses it differently. I know that now. I was still mixing the foods I liked with low-fat selections.

It wasn't until I moved back home after graduation that I made health (not weight loss) a priority. I hired a new trainer (Yeufre; you can see him in my Instagram stories), worked out three days a week for an entire year, and ate smaller portions. Also, just being back in New York City made a difference. I could walk everywhere. In college I was basically walking from the dorm to class to the library and back to the dorm. NYC was my playground to walk around in! I was studying so much in D.C. that I was just sitting all the time and had limited natural exercise. Finally, post-grad, I found a winning combination of the changes I made and saw strong results.

These changes didn't happen overnight though; to be realistic, it took a few years of a stressful job and a healthy exercise and food program to get into the best shape of my life and back to feeling confident wearing clothes beyond leggings and sweatshirts. A friend of mine once told me to be careful when wearing leggings because they are almost too comfortable, and it's easy to eat as much as you want. Quite honestly, those clothes make me a little uncomfortable now. They take me back to the years of my struggle and, like I mentioned in Chapter 6 related to purging and organizing your closet, you shouldn't own or wear anything that will impact your mood or confidence. All of those college clothes were either sent to a consign-ment store or given away. As a graduate trying to make waves and achieve her goals, there was no room for memories of these haunting times.

To note, I'm not a hundred pounds like I was when I started col-lege, but I still lost a lot of weight and have never looked thinner or felt better! It really isn't about the number, but how the weight is distributed, and, as we know, muscle weighs more than fat. It's almost scary looking back at how naive I was in my food choices. Even sadder is how upset I was at myself: how much I hated looking in the mirror and getting dressed in the morning. It still hurts when I get random direct messages from women on Instagram today, almost weekly, criticizing my weight, one writing that I have a "fupa"; another that I'm chubby. I've found that the better I look the more girls are being catty and making my weight a topic of their conver-sation. I believe women should be supportive of each other and not putting them down. It's so disappointing to see this happening. It's frankly body-shaming and cyber bullying.

Today, I focus on what and how much I eat. While not obsessive, I avoid foods that result in binge eating and try to be healthy each and every day. I never eliminate my favorite chocolate candy or choco-late chip cookies. But I do stay away from the dreaded cupcakes and maybe only indulge in one (typically mini versions from Baked by Melissa) a few times a year. I definitely have cupcake anxiety—eek!

I work out as much as I can, which is sometimes difficult with my career, but I don't get upset with myself anymore. I just strive to improve and have a more consistent workout schedule, when pos-sible. The point of my cupcake story is a lot of us have experienced or are experiencing a struggle with how we feel about our bodies. Just because we might not be in what we view as our ideal state of being doesn't mean we're not worthy of looking great.

Aiming high is all about *still* wearing incredible outfits, dress-ing up, and showing up every day for your present and future self, because no one else is going to show up for you. Living a balanced life is critical and creates a spiral effect from your health right down to your clothing choices. Today, I'm way more confident in what I wear because I know I'm a work in progress. And when I throw on a pair of heels, they make me feel unstoppable even when I eat too many cupcakes and all I have on is a pair of biker shorts and an old tee.

10.

DENIM DISTRESS

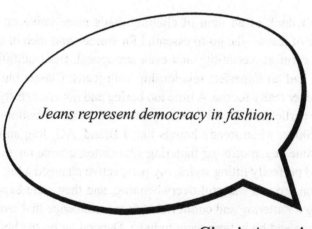

Jeans represent democracy in fashion.

—**Giorgio Armani**

10.

DENIM DISTRESS

I can't think of an item of clothing that's more universal than a pair of jeans—the go-to essential for women and men of all ages for comfort, versatility, and even sex appeal. But truthfully, I've always had an imperfect relationship with jeans. Classic blue jeans were never really for me. A little too boring and not enough style, and I never particularly loved how they framed my curvier bottom. In the early 2000s, when trendy brands like J Brand, AG, Rag and Bone, and Frame began offering flattering silhouettes, a wide range of colors, and perfectly fitting styles, my perspective changed a bit, but the selection process was still overwhelming, and they were expensive! Finding a flattering and comfortable fit is a challenge that women of every age and body type seem to have. Depending on the brand, my size might fluctuate between a 24, 25, or even a 26. It always depends.

I had a funny (well, not at the time) denim experience when I visited Israel in 2010. I found an amazing pair of jeans that screamed my name in a small boutique. Not your basic pair of blue jeans, though; rather, they were a light wash denim with black leather knee padding that made for perfect edgy day-to-night jeans. I had to have them. (How outdated those jeans must sound now!)

Calculating the price at fifty dollars, I paid with my credit card, but soon discovered that over twelve hundred dollars was charged!

Clearly with the language barrier and money conversion, I misunderstood the price. I tried to return them, but the store refused, claiming a no-return policy. Naturally, I was devastated and couldn't believe I did such a thing. Talk about lack of communication. No matter how much of a fashion lover I might be, I'm in no way, shape, or form, an irrational buyer. Yet, I had just spent my entire personal savings on a single pair of jeans!

While this was a ridiculous situation, they soon became my favorite jeans, and I literally wore them nonstop for years—that is, until my body changed, and I donated them to a good cause. Although guilty about my mistake, they really were a stunning pair of jeans.

This experience made me interested in where the denim trend began. Thanks to trusty Google, I learned that we can thank Jacob Davis and Levi Strauss for this wardrobe creation, as both were credited with inventing jeans. The utilitarian pant, which is made of a durable fabric, was first worn by physical laborers in the late 1700s. In 1853, Davis and Strauss formed a company called Levi's—today, an iconic fashion brand. Since that time, denim has additionally become a fashion item not just limited to that faded blue fabric. There are unlimited options today and selecting the right one for the desired purpose can be challenging.

Although Levi's are still a favorite with blue jean lovers, their classic jeans set the stage for many new denim dedicated fashion brands who gained popularity just for denim. After the J Brand and AG type brands that I mentioned above, top fashion houses also began taking it to the next fashion level, with collections by Balmain, Versace, and others. As a result, our choices are vaster than ever, and the price range is wide, from inexpensive styles under twenty-five dollars to hundreds or even thousands of dollars!

My perspective on denim changed again when I arrived at my freshman year dorm at George Washington University. Well aware that I would have only one small closet for hanging items, along with room for storage boxes under the bed, I *still* brought a ridiculous amount of clothing (to no one's surprise). The space constraints made the average NYC studio apartment seem quite large. Since New York was only a train ride away, I planned on returning home during school vacations and switching out my fall clothing for wintry outfits once the colder weather arrived.

Entering the dorm room on move-in day, I met my new roommate along with her stacks upon stacks of trendy jeans. I had a boatload of clothing, but this was insane—nearly a hundred pairs! Even more unbelievable, they were all an identical blue denim shade and an identical skinny silhouette pattern, with the exception of a single bright cherry red pair. Needless to say, this turned out to be the most interesting roommate experience I could have ever expected, and she taught *me* so much about the different ways you can dress denim.

Armed with this knowledge, I decided to give denim another try. What worked for me: shopping the denim departments at local stores and trying on pair after pair to discover what worked best. This is something I definitely suggest you doing, too, especially if you have a lukewarm relationship with denim. Trying on numerous options in the dressing room is a must. Your online purchases will be more effective once you determine your personal preferences. Learning what works and what doesn't, like with any other clothing item, is easiest when having an array of options right at your fingertips.

While I own a few pairs of jeans and like having them to alternate with trousers and skirts, especially on the weekend, I've never been one to necessarily run to purchase the latest trending denim style. It's actually probably the item I buy the least of. However, the denim obsession seems to be super strong amongst women and is especially applicable to my mom's sister and her daughter. They're the most denim-loving shoppers I know! Whenever my cousin and aunt visit NYC, they rush to purchase a new pair of jeans. During one such outing, my cousin Abby purchased several pairs, which I found perplexing. When I mentioned that she owns more jeans than almost anyone I know (with the exception of my former roommate), she laughed it off. But her mom turned quite serious, explaining that she often tried on four pairs of jeans in the morning before she could find the right one, so when new styles come out, she's always eager to see if there's something that fits or looks better. My aunt has retained the same body shape since high school (even four children later!), yet a pair of jeans, she tells me, can look and feel different, depending on her mood or spirit. So, options are key for her. Ultimately, I guess it's like any item of clothing or accessory—when you have an obsession, you pay closer attention to what's trending and want more to select from.

When you're shopping for the "perfect" pair of jeans, you want to be honest about your body. Shapes cover a wide spectrum, including hourglass, round, rectangle, triangle, inverted triangle, straight, and voluptuous. Fortunately, you can find a wide assortment of jeans that contour to your frame. I actually never realized all of the details involved in choosing the right pair of jeans.

First is the silhouette: There are so many different rises and shapes. Even jean legs—so many options! Skinny, straight, boot cut, flair, baggy, or wide. Yikes! The silhouettes that we commonly see year after year include skinny, straight, loose, boyfriend, baggy, paper bag, wide leg, and cropped. Although there seems to be a particular style that the fashion industry pushes each season, it is fair to say that anything goes and it's really about your comfort level.

The "rise" means where they fit on your upper body, waist and hips. There are high waist, medium rise, and low rise of where they sit on your body. Some people like the high rise to cover the belly while others find that to be too constricting. Although I like to be comfortable, to be frank, that isn't my first concern. Some people prefer a pull on or stretchy fabric, but I like body contouring support to make it sexy. The high waist is my personal favorite silhouette because it's elongating and also looks great with both tucked in tops and bodysuits, as well as cropped tops.

To add more choices, jeans no longer just come in denim or various shades of blue. The blue shades go from basic denim blue, light, medium, dark, washed, tie dyed, black, vintage, pale colors, and even bold colors. It is endless. The jean fabric can be denim but with patchwork, slightly ripped, or major holes and rips. The varieties are endless. All in the name of fashion!

Department store shopping is ideal for creating a great denim wardrobe because every brand is represented. It's also helpful to take advantage of the salespeople's expertise. They have experience watching customers try on jeans and tend to know the fit and what would be right for different body types. Unfortunately, it takes a lot of experimenting to see what works great. Most people, once they find their favorite brand/style, tend to wear those pairs over and over again.

Although some believe you can never have too many pairs of jeans, it's important to be practical. Four is an ideal number. A comfy pair (can even be a denim jegging) is ideal for daily wear, along with a cleaner, nice-fitting pair if your work environment allows you to wear denim to work. Sexy jeans, tight fitting and body sculpting, are perfect for date nights, and perhaps slightly ripped black jeans and novelty jeans can be a great deal of fashion fun. I still recommend if you tend to love jeans as part of your wardrobe that each year you take a look at what's trending and if it would be a nice addition to your wardrobe, just go try it and then make the purchase if it does, indeed, look great on you.

My relationship with denim has ebbed and flowed throughout the years, but following these tips for buying jeans and maintaining four basic pairs for different occasions has made it so much easier. Next time you're feeling stuck in a clothing rut, try looking for a new style, silhouette, or wash for your jeans. A simple shift can make a huge difference in your wardrobe.

11.

THE NEW RULES FOR WORKPLACE DRESS CODE

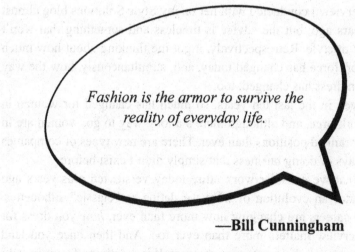

Fashion is the armor to survive the reality of everyday life.

—**Bill Cunningham**

"Women should wear clothes that make them feel strong and confident," designer Diane Von Furstenberg once told me. "At work especially, I think a woman should be comfortable." DVF discussed the importance of dressing for the workplace in an interview I conducted with her on my Style Solutions blog almost ten years ago, but the advice is timeless and something that won't go out of style. Retrospectively, it got me thinking about how much the workforce has changed today, and, simultaneously, how the way women dress has changed, too.

Even in the last ten years, so much has changed for women in the workforce, and although there's a long way to go, women are in higher ranked positions than ever. There are new types of companies and ways of doing business that simply didn't exist before.

What we consider work attire today versus ten plus years ago illustrates an evolution of what we define as "classic" silhouettes. While careers are changing now more than ever, *how* you dress for an interview matters more than ever too. And then once you land that dream job, how you present yourself is a defining factor in your career path.

Therefore, stakes are high and what to wear for your career has never been more challenging. After all, traditional jobs are dwindling, and self-employed professionals typically work from home. What's appropriate for one field or job isn't for another, so it's important to be cognizant of the differences. I'll dig into specific careers and corresponding best wardrobe practices later on in this chapter.

But first, my interview with Diane Von Furstenberg reminded me of some of the ways in which my closest family members have styled their work wardrobes throughout the years. Together, they've inspired me in my own career and I hope seeing a snapshot of how they dress for success will help you in yours.

MY GRANDFATHER

From my earliest memory, I recall my grandfather wearing a suit and tie to the office and essentially everywhere else. He was always dressed up in classic navy blue, white, and tan colors. He never wanted to stand out. As the brains behind his self-made business, his wardrobe choices reflected his desire to blend into the background. When traveling on a plane, he *still* dressed in designer suit and tie, to ensure respect. Quality was important to him. His Brioni, Turnbull, and Asser shirts, ties, and suits are ingrained in my memory.

The only time he relaxed his dress code was on Saturdays, when he wore a long-sleeved sport shirt and khaki-colored pants to the office. He traded out his jacket for a cashmere cardigan in beige or navy. Regardless of the occasion, he always looked professional, which was truly the essence of who he was. My grandfather worked in real estate and thrived in the field. He loved going to the office every day, but was still a full force family man who loved being with my grandma, his daughters, and eventually me and my cousins, his grandchildren. Everything he wore was always soft, symbolic of his sweet personality. Hugging him was the best feeling because he had a distinct scent that was always so fresh and delicious smelling, and that was thanks in part to his clothes. I can still remember that smell and touch of his clothing today.

MY FATHER

As a dermatologist, my father always wore a white coat over his clothing when meeting with patients, but he also wore a suit and tie underneath. However, about five years ago, dad took on the "hip" dermatologist look of casual black pants and a black sweater. As his clothing shifted, so did his dermatology practice. In the last five years, they've evolved to appeal to a younger demographic, as reflected by my father's work wear change.

I feel like for doctors, lawyers, bankers, and other professionals who are dealing with more serious matters of their customers' or patients' lives, it's more comforting to see them polished and dressed up. It still makes me a bit uncomfortable to see my dad in his new work uniform, because I still envision him in more formal attire, but he wants to look "cool." We constantly go back and forth on this topic.

MY MOM

When my mother started her career as a buyer at Lord and Taylor, women were not allowed to wear pants to work, only skirts and dresses. It was very clear. But once Bill Clinton was elected president in 1993, with Hillary Clinton adopting stylish yet comfortable pantsuits as her fashion brand, professional women began wearing them regularly.

My mom's career transitioned into the beauty and medical worlds, and eventually she was running an Israeli technology company's North America subsidiary. I recall her struggle to pack the right clothing for her first trip to Israel for a 2009 board meeting. She wanted to be culturally appropriate yet consistent with her style. In this case, she thought she needed a little help, so she asked the personal shopping department at Bergdorf Goodman for guidance. Since it was mid-summer in Israel, with temperatures both hot and humid, the personal shopper recommended summery fabrics and colors. Arriving at her first meeting, my mother was flabbergasted to see the men in denim jeans and t-shirts and the lone other woman in the room (who was with the venture capital investment firm) dressed in head-to-toe black designer clothing by Marni. It goes to show that even when you plan and do your fashion research, sometimes you might not always get it right. However, it's always best to play it safe when dressing for a new job and go for more formal, conservative outfits until you can get a sense for the office style.

ME

My "work" wardrobe certainly has evolved from my days of being behind the computer screen to in front of the television camera. Even though I worked as a fashion editor, I still felt I was a representative of the company I worked for even though I didn't want to stand out too much. I always accessorized with fun little purses and high heels, but in terms of the clothing, it was definitely simpler than how I dress now. For my career today, my purpose is certainly more focused on standing out. So, I have more fun with cutting edge silhouettes, bold patterns, and bright colors. As I always say, your wardrobe is truly a reflection of where you are in life, so as your career is shifting, your outfits will, too.

DRESS UP OR DRESS DOWN?

Recently, I've heard the line that men in suits work for men in t-shirts or hoodies. In fact, Facebook founder Mark Zuckerberg often wears hoodies and jeans (along with every other tech bro). Of course, this has extended a bit to women in the start-up/tech world. A good rule of thumb if you're in the start-up world: jeans are probably a "go," as long as you still look put together. After all, we are living in a free-wheeling and relaxed fashion era.

On the other hand, if you're in a traditional profession like law, finance, real estate, or banking, it's likely that the dress code hasn't changed much since my grandfather's day, with some adaptation for business casual days (first implemented widely in the '80s). You're still expected to dress in more formal attire with strict guidelines, which can extend to lengths of dresses and skirts to certain acceptable colors. If you are a courtroom attorney, for example, very formal attire is still expected, regardless of gender.

In a creative field like fashion or entertainment, you have more room to express your personal style and have fun with your choices. It really all depends on your field and your company's unique culture. Feel free to take bigger risks with silhouettes, colors, and patterns, but remember to keep it professional.

Of course, there's been a major growth of social media influencers too, who have endless work wear options to choose from. For some millennials, their careers are entirely driven by advertisement or partnership revenue from Instagram or Tik Tok. These "influencers" reveal themselves to the world nearly twenty-four/seven, which requires constant vigilance of how they present themselves. If you're someone who posts outfits on Instagram, you should feel totally confident in what you're sending out to the world. Everyone from a potential date prospect to your new employer can use it as a way to get to know you better and see how you present yourself. There's always the question of how much is too much? Is it OK to post lingerie, if tasteful? A swimsuit? How sexy is *too* sexy? There are so many elements to consider, but setting boundaries and knowing your own career goals is unique to each individual.

Some Instagram influencers are more candid than others. Look at "Real Housewife" turned Skinny Girl entrepreneur Bethenny Frankel, for example, who gives us a glimpse into her life at home through her Instagram account. She regularly appears without makeup and in pajamas, or trying on her Skinny Girl outfits and then glammed up for an appearance or date night. Frankel truly doesn't care how she looks or what she's wearing and just presents the version of herself that is live in that moment.

Being authentic through style on social media is something that takes confidence and a feeling of security that what you do won't have a consequence. More and more fashion influencers seem to be bringing this more authentic side to their posts, showing followers a variety of dimensions to their style as well as beauty routines. This all ties back to the new rules for dressing at work. As the definition of "work" continues to evolve, it's interesting to look at how we should evolve and "brand" ourselves via social media and IRL.

A note on job interviews: Although formal attire is no longer the rule for job interviews, you should still consider the position and work culture environment. The surge of millennials working in the new gig economy has blurred the lines a great deal. The company interviewing you might not have a local office or even an office in the same state. For many, the local Starbucks or shared office space like WeWork has replaced the traditional office. As your own boss, you can determine the dress code you want. Be sure to do your research, determine the type of company (law, real estate, start-up, tech, etc.), and then refer back to my guidelines above.

With my career, it's all about dressing for event and television appearances. Appearance coaches and stylists are available for the news anchors and hosts, but not for me. My outfits are expected to be on-trend, but not trendy. That is, dressing current, but looking like I didn't try too hard. As the style expert, I'm expected to set the tone for savvy trends, and all eyes are on my personal choices.

My global tip for workforce dressing is to understand your work culture and standards. Are jeans permissible or not? Is a certain type of clothing acceptable on desk days but different for meetings and/or outside events? Gather as much intel as you can during the interview and on-boarding phase. Make sure there is never too much skin showing in a professional environment, unless you are on the red carpet for your Oscar nomination. Your clothing should be clean and flattering. This also applies to your accessories—make sure your shoes are scuff-free and well-fitting.

Ultimately, no matter what career path you embark on, it's important to define your professional style so that it's reflective of what you're doing. What you wear is in many ways symbolic of the type of person you are, your interests, and your goals. Staying true to yourself while also staying aware of how your wardrobe choices can impact your career is critical. But with all of these tips, you should be ready to land (and keep) the job you want in no time!

12.

FASHION'S FOUNDATION: WHAT'S UNDERNEATH

> *The thing about fashion—it's like ducks going quack, quack quack. It's being dictated from above, and it just makes me want to rebel against it.*

—**Sara Blakely**

It was 2007, I had just turned thirteen, and my Bat Mitzvah was just days away. As a young fashion guru, this was my time to shine. I had a light champagne-colored custom Vera Wang dress ready to go for my service. It fit like a glove and took months to create. Just one major problem: I had just gotten my period.

Somehow, this always seems to happen to me—my time of the month always falls on the most important days. I felt super bloated on the afternoon of my big day, and my form fitting dress *definitely* wouldn't hide the pouch of my stomach. You can probably imagine the teen hormone-fueled meltdown that followed this realization. Luckily, like always, my mom said she had the perfect solution.

She introduced me to my first pair of hi-rise Spanx underwear and my life changed forever. I'm sure anyone who's had a Spanx "a-ha" moment can relate. When trying the underwear on, at first, they reminded me of scary granny panties. Seeing the fearful look in my eyes, my mom told me that my concerns would quickly disappear once I put them on. If this meant that I wouldn't feel as bloated in Vera Wang, it would be a Disney fairytale come true.

After slipping them under my dress for the first time, I remember seeing a huge difference in the mirror. It was magic. It wasn't about looking or feeling skinner—although many women feel this way—I just looked *smoother*. Instant gratification at its finest! I wasn't sure I would ever take them off.

When looking in the mirror, we're confronted with many conflicting thoughts. Sometimes they're realistic, but at other times, they are unrealistic and even exaggerated. Self-image jumps to the forefront, whether our weight, skin, or hair—the list goes on. Sometimes we're confident with our bodies and what we define as attractive, but in other moments, our deepest insecurities arise.

One of the most common remarks I hear from my friends regarding their looks is the lack of a perfect flat stomach. My reaction: No one is perfect, and what *is* perfect anyway?

Society's expectations are pushed to the limits when stars like Emily Ratajkowski or models like Gigi and Bella Hadid or Kendall Jenner are portrayed by the media as the world's most gorgeous women. They are all tall, skinny, and can fit in just about any article of clothing, straight off the runway—perfect for models, but hardly a reasonable standard for most to obtain.

Simultaneously, in this Kardashian-saturated world, the standard of what's "hot" also consists of an ultra-thin waist paired with a bootylicious backside and large boobs that are at least a C-cup. And these women tend to have one thing in common that my friends keep talking about: that envious flat stomach.

It's only natural to want to look like these stars. After all, their beauty is thrown in our faces twenty-four/seven. Some women eventually get over it, while others are just getting started. Although pricey, women sometimes opt for extreme procedures like liposuction, which is more instantaneous than going to the gym regularly.

So, when does a young woman's obsession with her body typically begin? It's different for everyone, but the usual onset is around middle school. I saw this with my own friends. The body negativity starts young. This baffled me then and baffles me even more today because it's normally when women are in their best shape. But with sex hormones on the fritz, weight and body shape often fluctuate, sometimes dramatically. These hormones can also have a major impact on mood, affecting how women see themselves internally, too.

Whether it's a pouchy stomach, flabby thighs, or flat boobs, everyone has their fixation. Overall, I was happy with the appearance of my body in my teens—I could eat anything I wanted without seeing the negative results on my body. But once puberty hit, so did my period, and I realized that I wasn't so flat anymore. Over time, my abs disappeared, and my stomach transformed into what I called a kangaroo pouch. It took a long time to learn how to eat and exercise in a way that was right for me and my body, and I didn't lose the pouch overnight.

My social life was vibrant, even as a young teen. It was New York City, after all. I hopped from party to party on the weekends, where bodycon dresses were the norm. They were tight and form fitting around my body, and probably a bit too short, but I wanted to feel sexy after a long week of wearing my ugly plaid school uniform skirt. But depending on the month, the pouch reappeared, and a fashion solution was desperately needed.

Historically, women looked toward fashion for assistance in sculpting their bodies. Tight fitting girdles with wide belts of elastic were first adopted by European royalty, specifically men who hoped to reduce their torso and hips, but quickly became the rage with women across economic classes. By the late 1600s, corsets lined with metal or plastic to create a slim waist had replaced the royal girdle. But the girdle returned with a vengeance by the 1950s and beyond. For many years control top pantyhose was the only alternative, until Sara Blakley's invention of Spanx in 2000.

Spanx was a modern and comfortable way to achieve the sculpting of the past but an even smoother look in clothing of the present. I truly believe women of all shapes and sizes should be using Spanx and other comparable shapewear brands underneath their clothes. The right shapewear underneath helps the clothes on top to shine. Shapewear is so important for both me and my mom, who obviously come from different generations. I think every woman wants to feel their best as they put their clothes on, and shapewear helps create the foundation that is needed.

Spanx not only manufactures pantyhose, but Blakley's empire also includes leggings, other types of shapewear, bras, and lingerie. Today there are many other companies in this space who want to push, conceal, and basically hide one's bodyily imperfections, even if this means only temporarily making you feel totally perfect. Some of the other popular brands are Commando, Honeyglove, Venus, Shapermint, and Yummie. To no one's surprise, Kim Kardashian West has introduced her own brand called SKIMs, which includes body tape to lift your boobs for a flattering look in low cut tops and dresses. Kardashian West constantly shares posts of both her fans and celebrities all wearing her designs. Shapewear is one of those things that's universally needed among women everywhere, and the desire/need of these pieces creates a common bond that can bring people together in shaping body positivity.

After my Bat Mitzvah miracle, I purchased my own pair of Spanx pantyhose. My mom still wears them religiously and magazines and websites constantly reveal that they're the secret weapons of just about every major celebrity ranging from Beyoncé to Gwyneth Paltrow. As the years have gone on, women are increasingly living in a Spanx world—clearly why it's valued as a one billion dollar company. I believe every woman has their inner beauty and fashion secrets, as well as tips and tricks, that help build the foundation of their wardrobe. Shapewear is one of those things that a lot of us use, yet no one sees on the outside. If it's the secret weapon behind developing a strong sense of confidence with how we look in our clothes, it's definitely doing its job.

Now in my adult years, I'm even more reliant on Spanx and other shapewear brands. They're still as powerful—maybe more—as I've aged. A career on TV will do that to you. Since we tend to look ten pounds heavier when on-camera, Spanx provides a more professional and smoother look. When I'm in a pinch or on a budget, I can always find great fitting tights at drugstores. I love the options at CVS and will alternate between those and Spanx. Shapewear can be expensive, and if you're wearing tights all the time, they can snag, so you want to have options that aren't super expensive, or it will cost you a mini fortune every time you need to replace a pair.

When shopping for shapewear, regardless of the brand or price, I suggest trying different styles in order to determine the best fit. It's also important to determine which body part is your main concern:

hips, thighs, legs, stomach, or bottom. The shapewear today is so body specific that you can choose spots of concern that need that extra squeeze. Often women don't want to only conceal but also accentuate a flattering body part, and that's possible as well.

Sometimes women find their size a little too tight and uncomfortable for everyday wear. You can consider going up a size for coverage but more comfort. Yet for special occasions, you may want to deal with the extra compression to feel perfect. It will take some time to figure this all out, but it's worth it! Another helpful suggestion that doesn't cost anything is to take advantage of the salesperson in the lingerie department of your favorite department store. This might not apply to everyone depending on your go-to store, but salespeople tend to be experienced and happy to assist in this difficult process, just like with denim. Sometimes, you just have to ask. They will often measure your body parts and have a well-rounded understanding of which brands fit which body types the best. Nothing beats professional guidance, so it's worth taking the extra time with the expert for the best results!

However you choose to use it, shapewear is such a critical component to fashion. In the most literal sense, what you wear underneath your clothes makes such a difference. As I experienced on my Bat Mitzvah and in so many scenarios since for work and in life, wearing Spanx and other body shaping underwear has helped me to feel like my best and most confident self, and there is certainly no shame in this.

13.

YOUR INNER STAR: WHAT WE CAN LEARN FROM J-LO, KARLIE KLOSS, AND KYLIE JENNER

Confidence—it all has to do with how you feel about yourself—it's about projecting the attitude, I'm happy with who I am.

—**Jennifer Lopez**

For my fashion blog, Style Solutions, I constantly sought out expert advice during interviews about trends. As a young fashion journalist, I had so many questions: Who creates the trends? Why do celebrities have such influence over setting trends? And how does the public decide what to wear each season?

"I think you have to know what trends work for you," Melissa Rivers, *Fashion Police* co-creator and Joan Rivers's daughter, told me during an interview. "I always believe in hitting trends every year of some sort, but with a light touch," she added.

Actress and burlesque dancer Dita von Teese also weighed in on the topic with a different opinion: "I like to encourage women to find their own personal style and stick to it rather than trying to keep up with trends or coveting someone else's look. The truly stylish woman can appreciate the style of others, but she knows her body and herself well enough to invest in key pieces that suit her rather than trying to buy the latest thing."

It's interesting to hear different women's perspectives on following trends and personal style. Using celebrities as a style guide can help you discover your personal style, make your own fashion statement, and find inner confidence that will shine through your clothing. Ultimately, you should do what feels most true to you.

These influential talents, ranging from singers, actors, supermodels, and reality stars, are among the biggest fashion icons of our time and have the power to create and influence, including through the clothes they wear. When wearing a specific designer's brand, their impact is a powerful PR (public relations) tool. They influence fans in the trends they follow and items they purchase. Their audience—the public—is constantly listening and watching. Aren't you?! Today, it's easier than ever to incorporate some of that star power into your life by dressing, and consequently feeling, the part.

It makes sense that many of the most beloved brands tap celebrities to star in their campaigns and act as brand ambassadors. Obviously, this isn't new, but over the years, it's become more and more of a trend. For example, Emma Stone partnered with Louis Vuitton. She not only starred in ads for the fashion house but dressed exclusively in LV for red carpets and award shows over an extended period of time as part of their deal. Same goes for Charlize Theron, who had a longtime partnership with Dior; Rihanna for Puma; Justin Bieber for Calvin Klein Underwear; and recently Jennifer Lopez for GUESS?—the list goes on.

Whether you're Kardashian-obsessed—I know I've always got my eyes on what Kylie Jenner's wearing—or sparked by Gigi Hadid's street style, social media is making it easy to find out what exactly they're wearing. You can either look at their stylist's Instagram account, if they have one, and if not, many stars have fan accounts. Fans will literally spend the time to research what they're wearing to break it down for you. And due to the power of fast-fashion brands and e-commerce sites, ranging from Zara to Boohoo to Nastygal, many will come out with looks that are nearly identical to what the stars are wearing, but at a price we can actually afford.

I personally take inspiration from certain stars as well as the stylists who dress them. Some of the biggest stylists in the game include Law Roach (clients include singers Zendaya, Ariana Grande, and Celine Dion); Mimi Cutrell (models Gigi Hadid, Bella Hadid, and Sara Sampaio; actress Priyanka Chopra, etc); Karla Welch (model Karlie Kloss, actresses Olivia Wilde, Tracee Ellis Ross, Busy Philipps, Sarah Paulson, and more); and Elizabeth Stewart (Julia Roberts,

Sandra Bullock, Viola Davis, Cate Blanchette, and beyond). Mimi Cutrell, in particular, is truly a mastermind in finding unique red-carpet options that aren't always just a beautiful dress—she helped to put separates (crop tops and pants, skirts, etc.) on the map as well as discover smaller designers who have since blown up into huge talents due to the exposure.

Different celebrities represent different sartorial ways, so you can look to each one for a different style purpose. For example, as I mentioned, I love Kylie Jenner's style. I specifically rely on her for street-style weekend inspiration. I've learned from Kylie that clothing can be simple (a basic grey sweater and a great jean) but still be high fashion when paired with a star accessory. Think of it as elevated weekend casual.

Next on my style inspo list: I look to Victoria's Secret model Elsa Hosk for color combination inspiration. She pairs unexpected hues, like a lime green dress with a blue Prada Bag or a brown teddy coat with a pop of neon pink via a turtleneck underneath. Sometimes, it's easier to visualize how to create bold outfits that are more risk-taking when you see that someone else has been able to achieve the look successfully first.

For red carpet style, I love supermodel Bella Hadid and actress Priyanka Chopra. These stars are great to look toward when you have a black-tie event or cocktail party and are looking to change things up with your outfit.

And, of course, there's JLO, my ultimate girl crush. Pure Hollywood perfection. Sexy, cool, and simply a star when it comes to mastering that perfect evening look. There's nothing like a "Jenny from the Block" red carpet moment. You can always find her in a totally glamorous ensemble with sequins, sparkle, and full-on pizzazz, while also showing off her body (do you see how amazing she looks at fifty?!)

If you want to truly dress like a star, there are five steps I recommend:

1. **Make a list:** First, it's all about finding whose star style is most of interest to you. Do your research by scrolling through

celebrity street style photos on Instagram or sites like *Vogue* and start making a list of your favorites.

2.   **Narrow it down:** Think about what you actually like about their style. Is it the color? Silhouettes? Designers?

3.   **Start shopping:** Select a few items from your favorite celeb looks and start looking at websites for similar options. So, if you like Kylie Jenner's motorcycle leather jacket, Google "motorcycle leather jacket," go to the shopping section, and make sure your preferences are set to the budget you want. I usually put twenty-five to a hundred dollars.

4.   **Merge:** Start incorporating these pieces with items you already have so you're not creating a carbon copy of the celeb look you love but are instead merging it with your own wardrobe to create an inspired celeb look, not a copy.

5.   **Show it off!** Find somewhere fun to go in your new look, take some pics, and have a blast!

My television segments for E! are also helpful in recreating celeb style looks. They are always inspired by recent celebrity outfits— this is only natural as the network lives and breathes celebrity content and coverage! My E! looks are always based around a certain theme. Examples have included: how to wear one black dress for every holiday occasion; how to dress for every Thanksgiving scenario (Friendsgiving, meeting the parents, staying at home with your family), and more.

My favorite E! celebrity inspired segment was a Valentine's Day segment in 2020, where I presented four swoon-worthy looks for every scenario you could possibly need to get dressed for that occasion.

AFTER-WORK DATE

Kylie Jenner inspired an after-work Valentine's Day outfit. She had recently posted a picture on Instagram of her wearing a monochromatic red leather suit. I took that idea and made it approachable for women of all ages and body types by opting for a red power suit moment in a cotton, stretchy material, accessorized with classic black patent leather pumps, gold chain earrings, and a black circle clutch. The suit was just twenty-seven dollars (pants + jacket) and looked nearly identical to Kylie's ensemble! Since Valentine's Day fell on a Friday that year, I thought it would make for an easy look for working women of all ages who needed to head straight to their Valentine's Day plans from work, without time to change in between. Even if it's not Valentine's Day, you can always keep a little clutch in your work tote and slip it out once you get to your plans. Your date won't know you didn't stop home to change!

FORMAL DINNER DATE

For a formal dinner outfit, I looked to Priyanka Chopra's 2020 Golden Globes outfit—an off-the-shoulder Barbie pink gown by a designer friend of mine, Cristina Ottaviano—and emulated the look with a mini off-the-shoulder pink dress from a website called Boohoo, which retailed for just twenty-three dollars! Priyanka's gown for sure cost thousands of dollars, but no worries! You don't need to spend a ton of money to get that Hollywood star look. You can easily elevate your outfit with glamorous accessories. I dressed it up with a forty-two dollar pair of crystal heart earrings, which was an affordable way to get the look of diamonds, which Priyanka was literally dripping in. And of course, there is not a more festive shape to incorporate into your look on the day of love than hearts!

It's easier than ever to get a glimpse into the everyday style of our favorite stars. We no longer have to rely on *People* or *US Weekly* to release paparazzi photos of these celebrities as they grocery shop, head into dinner, or attend an event to see their outfits. Open Instagram and there we have it, the ultimate unfiltered access for fashion inspiration. And as you can see, you don't need to break the bank to create celeb-inspired outfits that let your personality shine through. As long as you know who to follow and where to shop, and don't go overboard, you can get the look and feel of your favorite celebrities' outfits in your own closet and stay on-trend no matter what.

14.

WTF IS BLACK TIE OPTIONAL? SHOULD I RENT THE RUNWAY? AND OTHER EVENT QUESTIONS

Fashion should be a daily convenience, not a daily chore.

—Jennifer Hyman, Founder
and CEO of Rent The Runway

I RENT THE RUNWAY?

Throughout life, there will be occasions where you need that *one* special outfit. Most recently, I was in desperate need of a monumental outfit for a monumental occasion: my twenty-fifth birthday in February 2019.

So many people I know love their birthday. They count down the months, days, and seconds until the clock strikes midnight on the day they were born. I was never really that person. When I was little, I definitely saw the thrill: birthday parties each year where my classmates came, each one tied to a specific interest of mine. I had an obsession with cartoons and characters, so naturally Mickey Mouse made an appearance one year, as did Arthur the aardvark, a Britney Spears look-a-like, and Chuckie from Rugrats. My teenage years were complete with small, intimate dinners with my closest friends at of-the-moment restaurants in NYC. The same kind of format took place in college in D.C., and for the years following graduation when back living in NYC, I usually would just celebrate with my family. But for my twenty-fifth birthday, I had this desire to do something bigger: hosting a late-night bash in Palm Beach, Florida, my favorite place.

Over fifty of my friends traveled from NYC, D.C., and L.A. to be there. As the "fashion expert," I felt it was important to be super clear with my dress code. The invitation read, "white and gold," which was also the theme of the décor of the party. Now you might be thinking, how would someone know to be dressy or casual? The time of the event made things crystal clear. My party started at 9 p.m., so I was clearly going for a late-night party vibe. The setting was also formal, which my guests knew. I suspected the men would be a little confused, so I wrote to them separately, suggesting that they could wear a suit with a white button-down shirt.

It was also super important for me to wear a dress that everyone would remember! I wanted to make sure it photographed well and wouldn't be by a brand that anyone could find when searching for options online or in a department store. Designer Cristina Ottaviano, known for dressing stars like actress Eva Longoria, models Bella Hadid and Petra Nemcova, and model and Twitter-personality Chrissy Teigen, dressed me in the look of my dreams: a strapless white gown with gold and silver sequin embellishments on the top portion of the dress. I went to her studio multiple times to make sure the fit was just right. I wanted to make sure the sequins were embellished in a spot that would be noticeable in pictures. I wanted to make sure that everything looked as perfect as possible. Everyone else wore short dresses—I didn't state a preference, but it actually ended up working out nicely because my dress stood out for pictures.

Whether it's a birthday party, anniversary, wedding, philanthropic gala, movie premiere, or beyond, it's likely that the event you're finding that extra special outfit for holds as much weight in your life as the Oscars or Grammys do for a celeb. As if figuring out what to wear on an average day isn't enough stress, I understand how you feel about fashion-stake occasions. They can be overwhelming!

The challenge starts with the party invitation. Do you start to sweat as you read the invite?! Translating a dress code can be as challenging as a foreign language. So many terms, so many rules—what do they all mean? For example, what's "festive attire" vs. "dressy casual?" Hosts can be so creative with party themes and dress codes that their guests are left in the dark. I received an invitation recently that declared, "black tie and dress in Raphael style." It was like trying to decipher the Met Ball "Camp" theme all over again.

If your party invitation doesn't specify colors or the silhouette you are requested to wear, the occasion probably calls for a more general outfit. Yet, you want to make a great first impression. Don't feel doomed—I'm here to spell things out for you!

Let's break down the most common invitation codes and how you should dress for them—from my POV (point of view), of course:

BLACK TIE—FORMAL, ELEVATED EVENING ATTIRE

Bring out the glam.

What You Should Wear: Whether it's a black-tie wedding, award show, gala, etc., and regardless if you're the host or a guest, black tie for men means a tuxedo is required. Women should follow suit, so to speak, with a version that is equally formal. You can't be too dressed up for this particular dress code. It's a safe bet to opt for a floor-length gown—steer clear from anything mini. Choose luxe fabrics that are beaded and embellished. Don't be afraid to go for a color. Jewel tones are luxurious and flattering on all women. I love a gown with a low back, or an off-the-shoulder silhouette. If you aren't comfortable with a full-length gown, you can always find a very dressy black lace or other special fabric in a short or tea length silhouette. Accessories should be formal or elevated—bring on the eye candy! Anything crystal-heavy or diamond-looking is a must. Dramatic earrings; statement necklaces; bold cocktail rings. This is your time to shine!

BLACK TIE OPTIONAL

You don't have to wear a gown or tuxedo, but your host won't complain if you do.

What You Should Wear: I know "hate's" a strong word, but I legitimately hate this dress code. It was used for a charity event that I was co-chairing. Obviously, the dress code wasn't my call or I wouldn't have allowed it. BUT, it really drives me crazy. If you want your guests to wear a tuxedo, just say it. A mix of guests dressed in both formalwear and casual wear can be quite awkward. I personally wouldn't wear a gown. I also wouldn't wear a standard cocktail dress.

I'd go for a mini dress that is just pure WOW. Something full of glamour. Fun cut-outs, cool colors, elevated embellishments. Go for a high-fashion moment—what a celebrity would wear to the Golden Globes or SAG Awards. Know what I mean? It also helps to look at the event location for clues as to what's acceptable. If it's in a restaurant, it's probably more relaxed. If it's at a museum, amp it up.

COCKTAIL ATTIRE—TRANSLATION, SEMI-FORMAL

As in, a chic, knee-length party dress.

What You Should Wear: Bring out your LBD (little black dress). Jazz it up with a statement clutch and high heels. Make sure your dress hits two inches above the knee at most. Don't show too much skin. You want to look elegant and sophisticated. During warmer months, go for light pastel/sorbet hues, like a baby pink with a classic nude patent leather pump. You can also bring out your inner Awkwafina here and rock an elevated pant suit that has a little pizzazz.

FESTIVE ATTIRE—BRING ON THE PIZZAZZ!

Have fun with it!

What You Should Wear: To begin, this is different from Black Tie pizzazz. This is a dress code we typically see used during the holiday season or at artsy cocktail parties and gatherings. For a museum late night bash in NYC, "festive" was the attire and I found a sheer long sleeve top and long skirt set that I paired with lingerie underneath. It was embellished with mini colorful stones. It had an avant-garde look but came across as high-fashion and cool. This is also a time to have fun with your jewelry with oversized baubles. Glitter, embellishments, and all of that razzle dazzle are very much a part of this dress code.

DRESSY CASUAL—MIXING DRESSY & CASUAL PIECES

The best of both worlds.

What You Should Wear: A healthy contrast of major glamour and edgy casual pieces are welcomed with this dress code. Think a strapless feather crop top (a big trend in the Spring of 2020) with a high waisted pant, or depending on where you're going, even a pair of boyfriend jeans with a statement clutch and sexy heel. This is the perfect time to go for eye-catching colors, like neons or pastels. I tend to see this dress code listed for dinner parties—a setting that certainly welcomes jumpsuits or separate sets in fun patterns and fabrics.

Remember, you don't always have to buy something new. Mix and match pieces you already own to create something unexpected. If you want to invest your hard-earned funds, purchase select accessories to elevate your look at a fraction of the price. I suggest having both a short and long black dress on hand in case of a last-minute event. It's always useful and removes the stress if you can't find something new and special. If you really feel like you don't have anything in your closet that's appropriate for the occasion, I suggest looking at rental websites instead of buying something that you'll only wear once. Chances are, what you wear to an event like a wedding, prom, or gala won't be worn again, or if you do, it could be long into the future.

I actually tried to re-wear my twenty-fifth birthday party dress for New Year's Eve that same year and it just looked wrong. Granted, it was just a little under a year later, but still, it was an eye-sore. Everything about it.

Rent the Runway is a rental site that I frequent. Rent the Runway isn't high fashion but still provides fashionable finds. It allows you to rent the clothes for a couple of days at a time, with extended options in case you're traveling. Depending on your budget and what you're looking for, it can offer you solutions that won't have you wasting an outfit for just that one special day or night.

Ultimately, looking back at my birthday, my outfit was a central element that led to me having a ball. I felt confident and sexy. I literally danced the night away, posed for pictures, and wasn't insecure about a single thing! One of the common issues with strapless dresses is you feel like it's falling down and need to pull it up. Not this dress— it fit perfectly, and I was able to enjoy my night worry-free.

A special occasion calls for feeling exceptional. Birthdays, weddings, graduations, and parties are the ultimate moments to Aim High. Wear those strappy sandals you wouldn't normally wear. Put on that lipstick color you think is too bold for work. Every day can be treated like a special occasion, but rare events are another level. Whether it's a party in honor of you, or in honor of someone else, make sure you're selecting an outfit that makes you feel as good as my twenty-fifth birthday dress did for me!

15.

INSIDE OUT: HOW TO WEAR CONFIDENCE

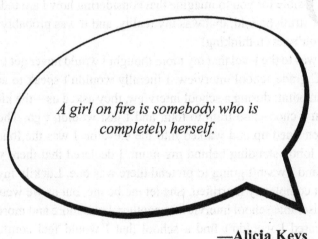

A girl on fire is somebody who is completely herself.

—Alicia Keys

During my childhood, I was painfully shy. It's probably impossible for you to imagine that considering how I am today, but truth be told, that was my reality, and it was probably worse than you're even thinking!

It was to the level that my mom thought I would never get through a NYC grade school interview. I literally wouldn't speak to anyone. Case in point: during a school interview, they asked us—the kids—to hop on a choo-choo train to tour, and I just wouldn't go. The other children lined up and walked into the elevator. I was the lone child in the lobby standing behind my mom. I declared that there was no train, and I wasn't going to pretend there was one. Luckily my mom wasn't completely mortified. She let me be me, but as we went from one miserable school interview to another, I was more and more upset and feared I wouldn't find a school that I would feel comfortable going to every day.

If that wasn't enough, I gave my mom an equally difficult time about clothing from a young age. I was beyond picky and the only outfits I would wear without a temper tantrum were a slinky, hot pink and turquoise long-sleeved dress or my personal favorite, a multi-colored dress featuring a bug and butterfly print. I can still feel its comfort thinking about it today. Of course, I also had to have matching faux lizard shoes with mini heels. Definitely a sight for the playground! I was truly so stubborn when it came to getting dressed. These dresses were the only garments I felt comfortable in and essentially became my security blanket.

Fashion ultimately clicked for me before I really even understood what it was as an industry and a potential career path. And it was the one thing that, as a shy girl, truly made me feel like myself, as well as comfortable with the ever-changing surroundings that I would be faced with throughout my childhood.

The head of the preschool that I attended admonished my mother for always sending me to school in "fancy" dresses and shoes. She constantly asked why she wouldn't dress me in pants or jeans like the other kids. Little did she know that this had nothing to do with my mother, as I already had my own idea of the clothing style I was comfortable in and would wear. And truly, I really hated wearing pants. I didn't like how they felt around my waist. I simply wasn't having it.

My mom was grateful that I eventually went to a grade school in a uniform, thus eliminating the daily stress, with the exception of the weekends when my inner Sydney would once again be freely expressed. Even then, I experimented with accessories. There are early photos of me with miniature stylish purses and sunglasses of all shapes and sizes—even adorable cat-eye frames, which is still my favorite sunglass style today. My mom and I shopped at all of the local kids stores, and she was kind enough to let me pick my favorites.

I quickly learned that clothing has a huge impact on how people perceive and treat you; both good and bad. I guess I always felt "dressed up" compared to most of my peers, but that's what I liked and how I felt my best. Being comfortable in your own skin is essential to feeling good about yourself, and your clothing choices send a message to the outside world.

Our clothes give a quick synopsis of who we are. Are we conservative or trendy? Interested in fashion or not? Bold and daring? Trying to get a cute guy to notice us? Or are you hiding behind your clothes hoping no one will notice? Do you care about being well-groomed and spend the time coordinating your looks, or do you use clothing to cover your body without thought? Do you spend the time required to make sure your clothes fit properly or are the pants just a bit too baggy and the shirt sleeves a bit too long?

Do we wear our clothing or does our clothing wear us?
Clothing choices can be indicative of your mood, the occasion, the weather, etc. These are all clues to our inner thinking for those who interact with us. Some people just don't care and that's also OK. If you do care, and I think most do, it can be overwhelming.

Recently I went back to the school that I attended from kindergarten through twelfth grade and spoke to high school students about my career. (Fortunately, the school did not require me to go on a fake choo-choo-train.) The current head of the school is a highly intelligent and knowledgeable educator. "Sydney makes fashion accessible through smart curation and articulation and critical analysis, something that really makes a lot of people, women, feel uncomfortable," she told the students, adding, "Many women question how they should look and how to afford it."

During my presentation to the students, I discussed how clothing dilemmas and challenges will surely change at different stages in life. I asked them the following questions and we had an intense, incredible discussion: "Do you dress just to fit in with others?" "If your friends are wearing jeans or a dress to that party, do you simply copy because it's easier to go along with the majority?" "Your friends might gravitate to a certain brand of jeans, sneakers, or handbags, and even expensive watches and jewelry. What if you can't afford these status symbols?"

It was such a rewarding experience to be able to share my knowledge with girls who could look up to me as a mentor. It's easy to talk about clothes and shoes on a superficial level, but so difficult to talk about how fashion choices can influence our confidence, mood, and feelings of self-worth.

Throughout my career, I have heard from countless moms who are working hard just to feed their families. They *still* feel intense pressure from their kids to keep up with every changing trend. These women sacrifice themselves just to make their kids feel comfortable in their clothing. This is a sad indication of what has happened in our society. Why can't we just be independent and comfortable within ourselves? Social media has only made this problem more visible and often people feel insecure if they can't join in with what everyone else has and is wearing.

But that's where my M.O. of being able to dress well and on-trend on a budget comes in. It's not about how much you spend or what brands you're wearing. It's first about the confidence that you bring out when wearing your clothes, and then it's about finding those pieces that help express your style and let you shine without having to break the bank to do so.

I have learned the hard way that you need to be comfortable with your choices and do what you want. If you love a style or a color and you want to wear it, just do it. So what if you want to wear purple from head to toe? Just try it out. If there's a big designer trend that is just too expensive but you genuinely like it, don't worry, because there's always a cheaper solution you can find.

It's so important to lead life in the way you want, right down to your wardrobe choices. After all, fashion is one way we express ourselves, and regardless of what you wear, there will always be someone who will criticize you. If that happens to you, next time, just think to yourself, who really cares?

16.

ACCESSORIES: WHEN TO INVEST AND WHEN TO GO TO ZARA

> *If your hair is done properly and you're wearing good shoes, you can get away with anything.*
>
> **—Iris Apfel**

I've always been obsessed with accessories. If there's anything that can make an outfit, it's a great pair of shoes or a swoon-worthy handbag. While I love clothes, I'm rarely on the "hunt" for a piece of clothing. Whereas for handbags, I usually keep a list of ones that I'm lusting over and want to save up for—I've been like this since I was a child. When I was a pre-teen I somehow managed to land a job as a salesperson at a clothing store in the Hamptons. I actually made really great money, to the point I was able to save up for my first mini Louis Vuitton bag that I wanted for what felt like years! That was the beginning of my handbag obsession.

Thinking about how women dress versus men, it always amazes me how easy it is for most men to get dressed. Think about it: with a quick change of a shirt or tie, they can wear the same suit day after day, and likely, no one will even notice. One season after another, they can get away with limited personal inventory. Women's clothing tends to be more memorable, which quite honestly, we want. However, the variety and volume of clothes a woman needs, and desires, can be impractical and financially unachievable. Guilty.

One thing I've done throughout my fashion career in an effort to extend the wear of my outfits is to repurpose my clothing by pairing it with great accessories. To this day, I love investing in a special piece for winter and spring, and in between, I surround myself with less expensive ones that I find from brands like Topshop and Forever 21. Some of my most recent searches were for the '90s collection of nylon Prada bags that were brought back for 2020. Another: the Bottega Veneta pouch clutch that was literally sold out for months, and then I *finally* found one laying behind a counter at Bloomingdales.

Ultimately, accessories are way more timeless than clothing. A lot of times in fashion, what's old eventually becomes new again. Look at the Fendi baguette bag—it was huge in the '90s, out for the last ten years, and now back again. My point is: your investment will go in and out of style throughout the years, and still become your go-to decades later.

I use handbags, shoes, and jewelry as my tools. The challenge: We often buy these items on a whim because we just love a pair of shoes, for example. Then we return home and realize that off-the-cuff purchase doesn't go with any of our outfits. It then fuels another purchase of an outfit to coordinate with those shoes, a domino effect that you didn't intend. Therefore, I believe you need to spend some time building your wardrobe from good solid basics that are wearable and timeless and expand from there.

What follows is my tried and true breakdown of how you should make purchases in different categories of accessories, what's worth splurging on, and what's worth saving on.

HANDBAGS

Handbags are difficult because there are so many options. When contemplating a smart purchase, you might think, should the bag have straps? Do I wear a backpack? Do I purchase a great looking purse even if it doesn't fit my cellphone? Or, do I purchase something practical? I struggle with this all the time, making impulse purchases like the trendy plastic see-through bags that look super cool in the store until you fill it with your stuff that is definitely TMI (too much information) for the public. I do need to have a tampon in my bag once in a while and for sure these purses aren't discreet—eek.

The holy grail of purses is a Hermès bag, usually a Birkin. The classic bag with handles is made of exquisite leather. The most popular color is still their classic orange but it's also available in black, taupe, red, shades of blues, pink—and any color or combination you want is possible by special order. Despite how glamorous this might sound, there are often downsides. First, the price. Even on secondhand sites, designer purses can cost over five thousand dollars and, in most cases, to get a new bag it's at least eleven thousand. Insane, right? Your home comes first, obviously!

One day, I took a trip into Hermès to learn a bit more, just for the hell of it. I learned that you can't purchase one off the shelf even if you have the money. You must be put on a wait list. The salesperson discouraged me from entering this race, explaining that there were about two hundred people ahead of me. Really? Then when a bag does arrive, you must go to the store and purchase it that very day. You can't even give a credit card over the phone and have it shipped to you. What happened to customer service?

Another high-end, inspirational brand is Judith Lieber, who passed away in 2018. She's the legendary creator of the minaudiere, or small decorative purse. The Metropolitan Museum of Art has eighty of her design pieces in their collection. These exquisitely detailed bags use stones and crystals in every imaginable inset and color, along with every possible category—from animals to books to women's lipstick. Some of her more recent hits, now spearheaded by creative director Dee Hilfiger (designer Tommy Hilfiger's wife) include a bag of French fries and an ice cream sundae with sprinkles. The Kardashians have given us a glimpse of these bags in their closets and they look like sculptures on their shelves. It is worth just Googling. The price range for her purses start at over a thousand dollars and go up for the more ornate and stratospheric custom designs.

The current desirable and more practical bags, while still costly, are Louis Vuitton, Chanel, Gucci, Christian Dior, Goyard, Fendi, Prada, Saint Laurent, Valentino, and Chloe, to name a few. I think it's great for your fashion education to see their new collections. If you can stretch for one of these bags, it is worth it. A basic black quilted Chanel bag with a gold or silver chain is timeless and will last you forever. Styles like that will never go out of vogue. The next upper tier but more affordable brands are Coach, Furla, Dooney & Bourke, Tory Burch, and Michael Kors. You can get a fine handbag from any of these brands. They are still costly but worth the investment and will be the foundation of your wardrobe. If you're looking to spend under fifty dollars, I suggest looking to Zara. Their bags are always on trend and made well. I also like Urban Outfitter's selection, as well as Boohoo's.

When it comes to handbags, I suggest keeping three categories of the best bags you can comfortably afford:

1. A great work tote, shopper bag, or backpack to fit your laptop, papers, or whatever you need for work.
2. An everyday purse that is fashionable and practical, most likely with shoulder or cross body straps.
3. A great clutch for your evening bag; it can be basic or ornate.

SHOES

When it comes to shoes, I definitely have a Carrie Bradshaw-level problem that is out of control. I can never seem to have enough shoes. As with purses, I think it's useful to remain on top of the designer fashion brands to view the styles and colors for each season. My "go to" designers are Christian Louboutin, Manolo Blahnik, Chanel, Prada, Gucci, Jimmy Choo, and Stuart Weitzman.

Since shoes, in most cases, are less expensive than high-end purses, invest in the best quality you can. If you can stretch for red sole bottoms (Christian Louboutin), do so in black or beige. If you can't, great options that are still pricey include Stuart Weitzman and the next level down, Schutz. A sexy sandal for your night out is also worth a splurge. I love a metallic option in silver or gold to go with everything. More expensive shoes last much longer, and plus, they always look on trend.

Focus on your individual needs and purchase shoes in the following categories:

1. A pump: for special occasions and last minute job interviews.

2. A fashion sneaker: to elevate an everyday look.
3. A strappy, sexy sandal: you never know when your Hinge date will invite you to a fancy gala instead of dinner and drinks.
4. Boots: a non-negotiable for any fall or winter wardrobe.
5. A flat mule: perfect for any workplace or great for dressing up denim.
6. A beach sandal: a needed alternative to rubber flip flops.

JEWELRY

The main jewelry categories as we know them are rings, bracelets, earrings, and necklaces. They can add glamour, a trend factor, status, and just complete your look. Personally, I am a costume jewelry kind of person because I like to wear the current fashion trends. They are more affordable, and I don't feel guilty making frequent purchases. I'm not someone who loses things, but if I happen to misplace one of these baubles, it's not like losing a thousand-dollar (or more) piece of jewelry.

With that being said, I still want to review some of the classic fine jewelry staples that you see on celebrities and influencers and have become very popular for all fashionistas. If you are inclined, have the means, or want to save for that splurge, I have a few suggestions.

The French brand Cartier has become really popular with their Love bracelets. They come in gold and white gold with diamonds in every width possible and have little screws going around them. Your loved one is supposed to gift it to you, and retain the key to unlock it. Unfortunately, the key often fails to work. Kylie Jenner couldn't remove her bracelet and the same thing happened to my aunt. Somewhat claustrophobic, this bracelet is a turn-off for me, but to each their own. It is also impossible to take it off each time you go through TSA security. You will likely be required to go through a second round of screening, but they are well aware of these bracelets.

Van Clef and Arpels also has been around for a while with their Alhambra or "lucky charm" collection that comes in many colored stones and remains popular. Hermès is also a hit with bracelets that make for a good investment. The most popular and classic styles are

Collier de Chien (the bracelet with history as a dog collar to protect hunting dogs). It is leather with metal and a few years ago was impossible to find. The Clic Clac H is the classic H bracelet with enamel and comes in different colors and widths. The Rivale is calf skin and does a double turn around the wrist. It has a metal pyramid and studs on either side. My favorites are enamel patterned bracelets in different colors and widths—gold, white gold, and rose gold—I've invested in a few. The original patterns have an equestrian feel (some with actual horses) to them. They can be mixed and matched and are just classic.

For less expensive options, I'm also a huge fan of Bauble Bar, a website that features amazing jewelry finds under a hundred dollars. Each category features trendy items that are high quality but low in price. As someone who likes to evolve with what's fresh and current, it's a great destination to shop as they too are releasing new designs as fast as we're talking about them.

Within each category of jewelry, there are endless possibilities. For bracelets, we see bangles, chains and charms, cuffs, and others. Recently stacks of bracelets became a popular trend. Earrings range from hoops to studs, drop, dangles, huggies, climbers, and crawlers. Necklace styles of the moment include chokers, collars, strings, and chains.

Don't rush to purchase a ton of pieces all at once, but rather, slowly build and evolve your collection to correspond with your wardrobe. Make sure you stay organized and keep your jewelry visible so you always know what you have. The right accessories can elevate any look and are the perfect way to bring out your own unique flair. Investing in higher end pieces will pay off for years to come—I *still* use my first summer-job- funded Louis to this day!

17.

YOU NEED A FASHION BUDGET

*Elegance is a statement, an attitude.
Elegant women are women of
character with confidence.*

—Elie Saab

17.
YOU NEED A FASHION BUDGET

It's often difficult and stressful to balance our personal budgets, and rightfully so. Your wardrobe isn't the first expense to come to mind. First, you need to allot for what is essential—the "musts"—like rent or car payments. After those needs are taken care of, you can start to think about the "wants." For some, those "wants" consist of clothes, bags, shoes, and jewelry. For others, they could be trendy home furniture or cool beauty tools. Our wardrobes might feel like they fall under the "need" category, and in some professions, like mine, this is actually the case. But usually, it comes down to what we *want* to purchase for the current season or for a special occasion. Don't feel guilty—you're not alone. We all have our thing, and that's OK.

When budgets are tight, the best way to feel fresh and trendy is to use your basic black tops and bottoms and add a seasonal fashion pop with trendy accessories that you can find on low-price websites and at stores. This trick instantly changes and updates an entire look to perfection. Another way is to make a new purchase—like a trendy silhouette—and then be creative with different ways to wear it.

I recently did a fashion segment for a newly launched nationally syndicated show on CBS called *Doctor and the Diva*. While there are always surprises when I get to each show, I got on set to realize that the "Doctor" of the duo was someone I knew as a child who worked with my father in his medical office, Dr. Steve Salvatore. The other co-host is singer Kimberly Locke from *American Idol*. For the segment, budget came into play in a major way. I was tasked with selecting one sweater—an oversized chunky grey cardigan from Zara—and styling it for four different women of every age and body type. Four models walked down the show's runway (ranging from ages twenty-five to sixty-five) in four different versions of the look.

First came Jonna, a plus-size model in her late twenties. I showed how she could wear the sweater to the office by layering it with a patterned blouse underneath and tucking into a high wasted pleated skirt. Next came Joan, who's sixty-five. She rocked the weekend casual look. The sweater didn't have buttons, so I closed it with a metallic belt to give it that cinched-waist effect. I paired it with a basic white t-shirt and jeans. For Hawa, a model in her thirties, it was all about showing how you could wear that same grey sweater to the gym or as part of an athleisure look. I coordinated it with a purple sports bra and leggings, sneakers, and a metallic fanny pack. Last, but certainly not least, Shirley, who was in her twenties, showed off how to wear this sweater for a glamorous night out on the town. She stunned in a sparkly silver and rose gold, sequin-embellished maxi dress, and the sweater fell just perfectly over her shoulders, acting as a shawl instead of a cardigan. This is just one example of how one smart purchase can be used and worn in so many different ways.

When we still don't feel like we have anything to wear, we always have the Internet. Shopping has become so accessible since we can do it twenty-four/seven on our laptops and phones at any time and any place—even in bed! This is simultaneously good and . . . not so good. Watching Instagram's fashion influencers showing their daily on-trend fashion picks might make your own wardrobe seem boring and stir you to start purchasing. When I post my daily #OOTD (outfit of the day) posts, it's not to make viewers feel that they don't have the right clothes, but rather to show how I would style pieces together and inspire you to make some of those combinations out of what you already own. If we swiped up every time an influencer or fashion personality linked to a shopping site for the outfit they're wearing, we would soon go broke. It's an easy habit to fall into and an impossible one to break once you get hooked. Even for me, as someone others look to for fashion advice, it's easy to become addicted to what some of my favorite influencers are wearing. Let's not forget—many of our favorites are being gifted these items, and I too get sent gifts very frequently. It's a perk of the job, but it's a reality to note.

So, how can you look great all the time, be on trend, and not break your bank account?

There are a few solutions that I suggest and that I personally incorporate with everything that I own and wear. Start by taking a good inventory of the clothes in your closet that you love (this should be easy if you followed my steps in Chapter 6 to purge your closet) and make sure to follow the below tips so you always look like a million dollars!

1. Your clothes must always be clean; no spots or stains or discolored fabric.
2. Everything should look as close to new condition as possible.
3. Make sure you don't have threads hanging and if you do just carefully snip.
4. When your sweaters have pills from being old or your purse rubbing against them, get a manual or electric pill or lint remover.
5. Make sure your clothes are never wrinkled; invest in an iron and even easier, a steamer. I have a mini travel one that I absolutely swear by and take with me wherever around the world I go.
6. Have proper fitting bras and underwear, since they're the foundation to your clothing. Don't forget—unsightly panty lines should not be showing.

Once you've completed the steps above, there are a few ways to approach building a wardrobe on a budget. I'm all about the core pieces (sometimes called capsule pieces) and you need to take some time to find what fits you best. You need a few pairs of pants that fit perfectly. I suggest a tight fitting pair for your thin days (like a leather legging) and a more comfortable pair for those bloated days—wide leg silhouettes with a stretchy band work. Stick to basic colors: a black, a navy, and a novelty plaid as your trendier piece, for example. A couple pairs of flattering jeans in different styles and a couple of skirts (a mini and a maxi) will do you wonders. Tops can be your "wow" factor, although it's great to have layering pieces, like tanks and bodysuits. I love Aritzia and Uniqlo for basic pieces at cost-effective prices.

Since I'm always asked where to shop on a budget, here is a rundown of my favorites.

DEPARTMENT STORES

Large department stores are my go-to destination for fashion trends and sales. You should browse their collections to see how their merchandisers style the clothing. Also, take advantage of the sales associates to guide you through what's new and how something should fit you. Often, you can find good bargains not too far into each season and then after the season they start at 25 percent off and keep going higher until they are sold from there. Remember that these top stores have their discount branches that offer the best prices at all times: Saks Fifth Avenue (Saks Off Fifth), Nordstrom (Nordstrom Rack), Neiman Marcus (Last Call), and Bloomingdales (Bloomingdales Outlet). These are always good places to check out to see what they have available. Also, their return policies are the most flexible if you get something home and really don't like it as much as you thought: it's easy to return without justification.

FASHION BOUTIQUES

ZARA

There is nowhere better to shop trendy items that are made well and fit great. They always have the best assortment of advanced fashion based on silhouette, fabric, and colors. They emulate high-end designer clothing at obtainable prices. They view themselves as a fast fashion retailer. They are always on trend and their clothes look more expensive than they are because they are made well.

H&M

This is another great option for either basic staples, or my personal favorite, their designer collaborations. Over the years, H&M has partnered with top designers and fashion houses like Karl Lagerfield, Moschino, Alexander Wang, Kenzo Roberto Cavalli, Versace, and Giambatista Valli. I've experienced some of my craziest fashion moments at their exclusive openings for these launches—something insane always happens. I have the opportunity of attending the preview shopping events before the clothes release to the public and it is unbelievable. The lines are still crazy and it's like a timed mini-shopping spree where security guards are monitoring you in every way. You can only purchase one of each item and have to be finished within minutes—this is to prevent people from reselling on sites like Poshmark and eBay. Quickly, everything is sold out until they restock with returns, but your allotted time is up.

ONLINE SHOPPING SITES

Online shopping is definitely convenient but don't underestimate the amount of time it takes to search and search for the perfect items. To add to the challenge, you really don't know how the items fit until you receive the package and try it on. The good news is most have quick shipping options; often two-day or sometimes next day if you're in desperate need (fashion emergency) and want to pay extra, and you can return or exchange. Make sure to purchase from sites that will provide you with a shipping label so you don't find yourself paying for return shipping, which may cost as much as the clothing item. This happens with many online retailers that are based outside of the United States.

Low Budget Sites

Boohoo

They have a huge assortment of clothing, boasting over 27,000 styles comprised of their own brands. Boohoo's customer is young and items are priced low with frequent sales up to 80% off. The assortment is wide and trendy, and to top it off, your order is complete with next-day delivery!

Lulus

Lulus was started by a mother and daughter as a brick and mortar store called the Fashion Lounge and the Shoe Parlor. They specialize in low price and sale items. Some items are their private label and some are other brands. You get 15 percent off your first order from their site and they offer tons of high style and low-priced discount clothing. I feature the brand in many of my segments.

ASOS

This is a British company that sells over 850 brands. ASOS is probably my favorite because it has nearly identical copies of all the high-end designer fashions. They definitely get the styles and colors on point. This site is also great for accessories: shoes, bags, and jewelry. A fun aside is their acronym: ASOS originally stood for As Seen On Screen and was meant to symbolize finding clothing that you saw celebrities wearing on your favorite television shows or films.

HIGH END SITES

Net-a-Porter

This is an online shopping site that merchandises the clothing to look like they're straight out of the pages of a magazine. Similar sites at this price range are Farfetch and Matches. Net-a-Porter features highly stylized designer clothing but is sprinkled with lower priced items. I think the lowest item I've ever purchased on the clothing front was two hundred dollars, so it's still pricey in the grand scheme of things. It's a great place to view the fashion trends and they do have great sales. In certain cities like New York, they offer same day delivery in a little car that drops off a shopping bag which has honestly saved me during last minute television appearances and events. If the item doesn't work, you can call and they'll pick it back up. Out-of-state customers receive their shipments through the mail but once again they are easy with returns. The best part: Net-a-Porter has a separate discount site called the Outnet that features clothing at daily discounts from 40 To 70 percent. The only catch is it's a season behind, but that's not bad for high-end designer clothing.

Shopbop

Launched in 1999, Shopbop has evolved into an e-commerce destination that features some of the coolest clothing, and to my personal taste, fashion accessories of our times. The company was acquired by Amazon.com in 2006. Every item is hand-picked from the industry's contemporary and designer labels. I love browsing their editorial look books and features.

Revolve

This is honestly where I shop the most out of any place. I love it because you can find both high and low pieces, but I mainly shop for clothing under $150. They buy in a very fresh, cool, and colorful way. The labels that I love most are exclusive to Revolve. There's new merchandise every week. Whether I'm looking for a night out look, casual attire, or just a fun costume piece of jewelry, there is always something I want. Revolve is also known as the hub for housing the clothing lines of the industry's top bloggers, like Aimee Song and Camilla Coelho.

We can't talk about fashion budgets without talking about the best rewards credit cards. I have found that you can save even more on fashion by making your purchases with a credit card like American Express. They have great points and awards programs that I believe are even more aggressive than the department store programs. You should spend some time to determine which card will give you the most for your money. Once you accumulate enough points, you can trade them in for store gift cards. There are so many options here! I tend to use these for my major purchases that would be unattainable without this type of financial assistance. I saved enough for a Gucci bag and Louboutin shoes through this method, so trust me, it's worth it!

When you're considering a big fashion purchase, it's worth restating that it's always best to buy a more classic special item that will last for years. Think: a quilted Chanel chain purse or a basic Louboutin in black or nude (not that there's anything *basic* about Louboutin). Versatile is what you're looking for when building your wardrobe. Ultimately, these will be the pieces that last in your closet for years to come, and ones that you'll find yourself gravitating to when figuring out what to wear as you get dressed each day. You'll see!

18.

THE DO'S AND DON'TS OF VINTAGE AND RESALE

I think we all know boldness when we see it. Nothing makes me smile more than when I see someone being fully themselves, with their own individual style and character, whatever that is.

—**Angelina Jolie**

OF VINTAGE AND
RESALE

The first time "old" clothes—a.k.a. "vintage"—appealed to me was when I first raided my Grandma Hannah's closet. Imagine: gorgeous tweed Chanel jackets in every color of the rainbow (in my size!), Escada blouses in swoon-worthy prints and patterns, and, my personal favorite, shoes—lots of them! Shoes, shoes, and more shoes. She could have owned her own shoe store. All of the hot brands of the '90s like Susan Bennis and Warren Edwards, more Chanel, and other top labels crowded her closet. My grandmother was reminiscent of Imelda Marcos, former first lady of the Philippines, who reportedly owned a jaw dropping 1200 pairs of shoes. It was definitely one of her obsessions. Over the years, I've caught onto it, too—big time.

My grandfather, one of the humblest men I have known, could never understand why someone would want to wear someone else's old clothes if they didn't have to. He tried to convince me to stop going through my grandma's closet and just buy a new outfit. He viewed clothing as highly personal—a part of your body and your personal history that should not be shared. It should be yours alone.

Yet today, retro, vintage, and resale/consignment clothing are all the rage and a booming business. Just look at the deals you can get: great fashion from the past at a fraction of the original cost, while also being environmentally conscious.

Millennials, in particular, are increasingly concerned with protecting our environment in every way that we can. The repurposing of clothing has become a statement at major Hollywood award shows. Jane Fonda famously wore a gorgeous red Elie Saab gown to the Cannes Film Festival in 2014 and then wore it again to the Oscars in 2020. More amazing is that her body's shape didn't change, and she looked equally as stunning. Actress Kaitlyn Dever wore a Louis Vuitton dress made with eco-responsible fabrics to the Oscars, and then paired the look to a budget-friendly forty-seven dollar pair of Aldo shoes. Starlet Saoirse Ronan opted for a black and lavender Gucci dress and the black fabric was made out of reused materials—materials made from waste is popular and truly a trend being taken on by celebs and beyond.

We're seeing other stars make a slight change to an older dress for it to look new as another way to be sustainable. Elizabeth Banks re-wore an Oscars *Vanity Fair* after-party dress sixteen years after debuting it for the very same occasion in 2020! She removed the elaborate bejeweled designs that were embellished over straps of the pre-worn red Badgley Mischka gown and instead opted for simple elegant spaghetti straps to give it a fresh and updated perspective and an ode to sustainability. We will definitely see more of this phenomenon in the future. It's great for the environment and equally as much for our wallets.

Resale fashion is a huge, growing market and includes the following range of categories:

Retro: This clothing could have been created over the past few years, but is influenced by trends that were fashionable in an earlier era. In other words, retro does not refer to a specific time period when clothes were actually made.

Vintage: Typically defined as items that are twenty to twenty-five years old. If the item was created by a high level designer/brand, ten years is acceptable. Think Chanel, Prada, Louis Vuitton—that level of brand. So even if the style looks old, it's technically not considered vintage if it was manufactured in the last twenty years.

Consignment: Clothing that someone else has owned, likely worn, and must be in good condition to be sent to a consignment store for resale. The seller receives a percentage of the sale which can be significant (like 40 percent!)—and much more if you send them lots of items and pick boutiques that have regular promotions for sellers.

The queen of vintage clothing is costume designer Patricia Field, the Emmy Award-winning brains behind the fashion in *Sex and the City* (SATC), and Academy Award-nominee for her work in *The Devil Wears Prada*. She is a true mastermind in costume design and styling. Field opened her own boutique on the Bowery in Manhattan in 1966 filled with her eclectic finds. The looks she created for Carrie Bradshaw, the leading character in SATC, are current and trendy to this day. They're constantly referenced in fashion memes and on the websites of popular fashion magazines. As discussed, I still watch reruns of the show and try to emulate those iconic Carrie Bradshaw looks. They're timeless. Some of Patricia's most popular Carrie moments included the tutu skirt and tank top combo that she wore in the intro to the show (iconic moment), a corseted satin gown, and a belted white boyfriend button down shirt, which she borrowed from Mr. Big's closet after an unplanned rendezvous in Central Park. Let's not forget her Fendi baguette bags and loads of Manolo Blahnik shoes. Carrie Bradshaw became so synonymous with the shoe designer that Sarah Jessica Parker, who played Carrie, collaborated with the designer on her own shoe line in 2013—exclusively for Nordstrom. The collaboration did so well that SJP opened shoe stores across the country. Crazy how a fictional television character crossed over into real life retail!

On the West Coast in Los Angeles—Melrose Place, to be exact—Cameron Silver opened an equally exciting vintage boutique in 1997 called Decades. When working as a fashion editor, I visited his boutique and wrote a story about him. Silver set the standard in vintage clothing for the top Hollywood stylists, celebrities, and the world's most popular fashion magazines. He has given new life to designer clothing and accessories. His store is still a very popular shopping destination. He also authored a stunning coffee table book called *Decades: A Century of Fashion*, which sits on a table in my home.

Silver made high-end vintage fashion clothing and accessories accessible to all—a way to incorporate beloved clothing into your wardrobe, guided by one of the most knowledgeable in the field.

A popular consignment store that I both sell to and purchase from is the RealReal, which launched as an online site and subsequently expanded to brick and mortar. Not your typical retail evolution. Sitting in the backseat of an Uber during a working trip to L.A., I discovered by chance that my favorite online resale destination was in fact a very large building. The RealReal had opened its first store. Founder Julie Wainwright started the company on her kitchen table in 2011. Renting a U-Haul, she personally picked up unwanted clothing from her customers. Her business soon exploded. The RealReal carries women's, men's, and children's clothing, jewelry, watches, fine art, and home décor. Shopping both online and in-store is easy. You will surely find a plethora of appealing items at good prices. Often, they have something you searched for in the past, but couldn't find or it was too expensive. The company now has three retail stores, nine offices, and millions of customers. Their motto: Luxury consignment "extends the life cycle of luxury goods." Their tagline: "The future of fashion is circular."

You've probably heard the phrase, "everything that's old is new again," and this is for sure applicable to fashion. Those *Dynasty* days of shoulders with huge shoulder pads are back, although updated with smaller and less padding, started around the 1940s. There are *Dynasty* characters Alexis and Krystle Carrington to thank for that! Fast forward to the runways in 2018 and once again shoulder pads appeared. This circular notion assists in making sure that clothing never ends up being wasted—what you end up giving to a resale site because you're not "into" it could be brought back as a major fashion trend in a short time and be sought after by customers to purchase again.

My personal experience and thoughts: Consignment is great for sending off clothing that you: A) loved but just wore too much; B) looks outdated to wear now; or, C) just doesn't flatter your figure anymore. These are all valid reasons to say goodbye to clothing in your closet or drawers. Working in fashion, I shop a very specific way. If

I want something that is trendy, I usually visit Zara, H&M, Forever 21, and before they closed in NYC, Topshop—which still has small areas in Nordstrom stores, but the selection isn't as trendy as when they had their own stores. I can part with items purchased at these stores—donating clothing to Good Will, for example, after wearing them to a point where I'm over it.

But, if I invest in something major and can no longer return it, the item no longer fits, or I never really liked it—I've improved in making such poor decisions—consignment is a great way to help others obtain fabulous fashion at a more affordable price and to receive a bit of extra cash in the process, which is always a plus. Designer pieces like a classic Chanel black purse with a silver or gold chain will remain in style far into the future. Taking care of such items and storing them properly is key. For example, stuff a designer handbag with tissue or old shoe bags and store it in the cloth bag it came in to keep it looking new.

I don't recommend that you dress head to toe in vintage fashion, but rather, try incorporating special vintage pieces into your modern style so it does not look like you are wearing outdated clothing. I like to mix my Grandma Hannah's Chanel jackets with fun, current costume jewelry and mix and match with denim.

With consignment, it's easier if you are aware of fashion trends and can pick out patterns based on year, season, and collection. Consignment sales associates are also very helpful in advising which season and collection the item is from, if you ask. You don't want to purchase an item you thought was from last year, only to learn that it is five years old. Better to know than not to know.

Also remember that vintage and consignment clothing should fit as well as new clothing. I don't care how much you love a particular piece. If it doesn't fit, don't buy it. This is also essential for shoes. I can't tell you how many times I see women in shoes that appear far too large or small for their feet. A consignment bargain is meaningless if you appear to be wearing someone else's clothing or accessories. As with all purchases, take your time to select not just what you love, but what loves you.

It's lots of fun to plan a day and go to a variety of stores to browse, try, and explore! Sometimes you just have that desire to go shopping and purchase something new or you need something for a special occasion. Whichever it is, it may be just a fun activity to go to resale and vintage stores that you have never visited and hunt for something special. It may be a designer brand that is too expensive to purchase off the rack but you could get a deal at a resale store from the likes of Chanel or Dolce & Gabbana or just a cool miscellaneous item, like a special jacket or coat in a luxurious fabric or great color. Again, take advantage of the sales associates who are familiar with their brands and the trends, and who will help guide you to their special finds. What one person no longer wanted can be your biggest fashion treasure. Don't be afraid to dig in!

19.

PACKING SURVIVAL GUIDE: HOW TO BRING FASHION EVERYWHERE YOU GO

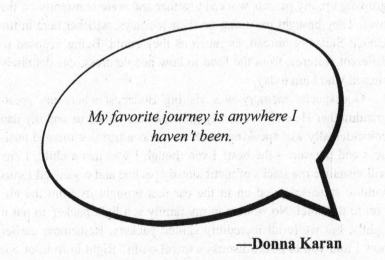

My favorite journey is anywhere I haven't been.

—**Donna Karan**

"How do you do it?!" is a question I frequently get from friends, colleagues, family members, and most commonly, my Instagram followers. When they ask me this, they're referring to my insane travel schedule.

Traveling has always been a huge part of my life. When I was growing up, my parents worked together and were constantly on the road. They brought me along on their journeys, whether here in the United States or abroad, as much as they could. Being exposed to different cultures, from the food to how people dress, has definitely shaped who I am today.

One special memory was visiting Budapest where my great-grandmother Helen is from. My grandparents joined us and my dad coincidentally was speaking there, so it was a trip that merged business and pleasure—the best! Even though I was just a child, I can still visualize the stacks of meticulously packed and organized Louis Vuitton suitcases piled up in the car that brought us from the airport to the hotel. No woman in my family is a light packer, to put it lightly, but we're all incredibly skilled packers. Remember earlier how I told you to never dismiss a travel outfit? Right in front of our hotel was Michael Jackson who was filming a music video for one of his albums. Thankfully I was perfectly fashioned for a photo opp.

Now, as a working woman in my twenties, it's my turn for business travel and frankly I have found it to be very rewarding. I feel super energized when I travel and love getting to network in different cities and work in a variety of environments. I love a little getaway with my family for some quality time too. But either for business or pleasure, traveling can also be a job that is frustrating and challenging. It requires lots of organization to make it easy once you arrive at your destination.

A couple of years ago, I had an exceptional trip that was neither business nor vacation. I was invited to a friend's daughter's wedding for a weeklong celebration in Dubai. This was going to be an extravagant affair with many events leading up to it throughout the week. In that country, weddings are held during the week and this one was on a Thursday night. In addition to the wedding itself, there were many other parties with different themes and in different places, like a Mehndi, also known as a henna party, where everyone got decorative designs on their hands and arms. This trip definitely required a lot of planning in the wardrobe and packing departments.

Since I hadn't been to Dubai before, and didn't know the customs, I took weeks prior to my trip to research what was and wasn't acceptable. Do I have to be sensitive to skirt lengths? Did I need my head to be covered? I really wasn't sure, but I knew that I had to plan each event very carefully. The only visualization I had was Carrie Bradshaw and her girlfriends going to Abu Dhabi in *Sex and the City 2*: colors, sequins, and full on glamour.

The night before the wedding was when the Mehndi took place and I needed to find clothing that was essentially a culture costume. I found an amazing store in the west village of NYC with gorgeous clothes from India and I found a beautiful skirt in orange with gold sequin embellishments that seemed totally fitting for the occasion.

For the wedding itself, all associated events I attended were for women only. In this culture, the men and women would be separated throughout the week until the very last few minutes of the wedding, when the groom would come to pick up his bride. So the actual wedding was all women and, like the saying goes, women really do dress for women! And let me tell you did these women dress over the top in the most gorgeous way possible—like royalty! I left NYC with what I thought would be enough outfits and then at the last minute I was invited to a fashion show for a top Dubai designer by a woman whom I met at the wedding. This event required something very special and the event space overlooked the entire city. So, off to the stores I went.

Normally people comment that I am always kind of "dressy." But this was the first time in my life that I actually felt I was underdressed compared to others' amazing attire, much of which was custom-made for the women. Overall, it felt very princess-like, and I will never forget this amazing experience that I was so appreciative to have attended.

Today, I am constantly on the road traveling to different cities throughout the country, all to pursue my dreams. When I first left my job as a magazine editor for on-air fashion commentating, my first regular gig was on a morning show in Chicago called *The Jam*. I was asked to travel there every month for nearly two years to host fashion and lifestyle segments on a budget. I was already accustomed to commuting, traveling almost weekly from my college campus to NYC by train so I could network at events and write for the magazine where I became a full-time editor upon graduation.

Knowing that Chicago is a major television market, I was super excited! Most people get their television start on local stations in small cities, so this was huge. As I mentioned before, traveling never exhausted me; it always inspired me—especially the interesting people I encountered along the way. I met the first guy I seriously dated on a train my freshman year. He was seated next to me and little did I expect but it went nonstop from there! When you want something so badly, you go the extra mile. Literally. By the way, I'm referencing my career, not the guy!

Now, I regularly travel to Los Angeles and Washington, D.C., among other cities. I'm in each place every few weeks. Many ask how I pack for all of my trips, both short and long. While we all probably pack with the goal of packing "light," the reality is, if you're going to invest in clothing, shoes, accessories, etc., you want to wear them as much as possible and just take everything with you. That's my belief, at least. Sometimes, that means packing a little extra than

AIM HIGH

146

you had initially planned, and enjoying wearing your purchases in different environments and destinations.

The worst situation is to travel to a location and not have enough clothes or the right outfit. I always pack a few extra items for that unexpected evening dinner, for example. I understand this isn't always possible, especially when you're on a twenty-four-hour work trip, or trying to convince a guy you just started seeing that you're definitely *not* high maintenance and don't need to bring a lot with you. I hear you! But, when you can, don't be afraid to bring along more than you need, just to be safe.

START WITH THE LUGGAGE

The first step to packing fashionably—and wisely—is to have a great suitcase. I will say, this is one item where I suggest splurging if you can. A great piece of luggage can last you for decades. I've had my luggage set since my high school graduation, and they've lasted me to this day. My luggage is from a NYC-based brand called T. Anthony. I have three pieces, each one between five hundred to a thousand dollars: an oversized wheel bag, a smaller wheel bag, and an oversized tote. If I'm going on a long trip, I bring all three and divide them by clothing, shoes, and accessories. They keep me organized from the get-go. This conservative and traditional brand is available in solid colors of canvas with brown leather trim. They come in black, brown, grey, red, and my special bluish-purple set. They also will monogram your suitcases free of charge—an old fashioned, fancy, yet quite trendy touch.

PACKING 101

How should you pack your belongings? I always pack my clothes on wire hangers. I don't want to spend my time in a hotel room putting them on hangers. I'd rather do that at home. Also, wire hangers are light and don't take up too much room. I ask the hotel to remove their hangers upon arrival and I just use mine. For my undergarments, pajamas, gym clothes, etc., I use clear packing cubes. You can get them at a store like the Container Store. They keep items from floating around your suitcase and getting wrinkled. It also feels more sanitary to put a bag in the hotel drawers as opposed to your undergarments directly touching furniture that many people have used. Germophobe or not, you feel my pain.

SHOES & ACCESSORIES

My shoes are kept in shoe bags with small shoetrees inside of them, so that they don't get destroyed. The shoetrees help to keep their shape. I also put my handbags in shoe bags. That way the leather or fabric is prevented from getting scratched or ruined. You can also put tissue or towels inside to keep their shape, but that does make them bulkier. Often I also pack a black felt tip marker in case I scuff my black shoes and need to do a quick repair.

PRE-PACK & PRE-PLAN OUTFITS

As the planner I am, I like to pack a few days in advance of my trip. Then, twenty-four hours before my trip, I revisit my suitcase to determine if I packed too much or too little. That way, I still have time to fix it. I like to plan out my outfits on my bed, pairing accessories with clothing in advance to avoid over-packing. For quick reference, I take photos and store them on my phone or in a special album that I keep at home. This is especially helpful if you know your travel schedule ahead of time.

DON'T FORGET YOUR EMERGENCY CARRY-ON OUTFIT

Another tip that I swear by when checking luggage is to pack an emergency outfit in your carry-on luggage. Be safe, not sorry. If the airline loses your bag or places it on another flight, frustration and embarrassment can ruin your trip. When you have an important meeting to attend and must look your best, an emergency outfit is a lifesaver. It's so easy to throw in a simple dress, a fresh pair of underwear, and a set of high heels in case a fashion emergency like this arises. Try to make it a transitional day-to-night outfit. I don't wish this upon anyone, but you will thank your lucky stars if an emergency occurs and you planned accordingly. This is especially critical if your destination does not offer stores you like or that are easily accessible.

If you master these simple travel tips, you'll be packing like a pro in no time. It took me years to nail this, but I promise putting the work in before a big trip pays off. By planning your outfits in advance, investing in durable luggage, and always having a backup option, you can be fashionable wherever you go, whether it's a trip to Budapest, Chicago, or Dubai!

Happy travels!

20.

HOW TO DRESS FOR ZOOM CALLS: A FASHION AND WORLD REVOLUTION

> *Challenges are gifts that force us to search for a new center of gravity. Don't fight them. Just find a new way to stand.*
>
> —Oprah Winfrey

In early March 2020, warning signs that New York City was about to change were flashing furiously in my face. This wasn't a change of seasons or style. It was something much bigger, one that I could already tell I wasn't used to. For weeks, underlying conversations grew louder about some type of disease or virus, which people called the novel coronavirus, or COVID-19.

Like most people, I had never heard of coronavirus before mid-February, but oddly enough my mom started mentioning it. She read some articles about couples on the Princess Cruise ship in Japan and didn't have a good look on her face, to put things lightly. When I Googled the term "coronavirus" for myself and learned how problematic of a virus it could be, I was concerned, but it all felt far away. First the virus spread in China, then on cruise ships, then Italy, and it was rapidly expanding its reach. Very quickly, I realized that my country, and more specifically my city, were about to be affected in a big way. Even dating suddenly became risky, especially if you didn't know someone's recent history. I started paying more attention to this new buzzword more than most people my age, at least so it seemed.

The way we dress often evolves with the times and reflects current events. In the 1920s, women wore flapper outfits to express their independence and shift away from oppression. In the 1960s, free-flowing silhouettes and funky patterns reflected the younger generation's cries for peace. But Spring 2020 marked a new state of the *world*, one that would bid adieu to socializing, traveling, going to work, and ultimately, our normal way of life that retrospectively we took for granted. All things considered, this might sound a bit trite: but as a fashionista, this soon marked a serious transition for my wardrobe. I quickly went from the girl who was all dressed up with multiple events a night to all dressed down with no place to go but staying right at home. This all happened just days after my busiest dress-up time of the year: New York Fashion Week. Looking back, that felt like my official goodbye to my old life. It also marked the introduction to two phrases we'd be hearing a *lot* of going forward: "social distancing" and "quarantine."

Life officially turned upside down. My brother's high school classes were canceled a few days before his official spring break as concern over COVID-19 grew, so my family decided to leave Manhattan for our home outside the city in the Hamptons. I can't explain the feeling when we packed our car and left, but I knew in my gut that something was really wrong. In the back of my mind, as crazy as it sounds, I was thinking of the iconic scene in *The Sound of Music* when the Von Trapps packed up to leave Austria. I couldn't get that vision out of my head. At the same time, though, I thought I'd be back in the city a few days later—first for a fashion segment on NBC's *New York Live* and then for a spot on *Good Morning America*, so I only brought a handful of clothes with me.

When I wrote this chapter, over three months after quarantine protocols began in New York, I still hadn't been back to my apartment in NYC—by choice, of course—for my family's health and safety. Quarantining and not having human contact with anyone but my family for three months IRL led to major lifestyle and wardrobe changes.

In those three months, my clothing choices had a complete reboot. I have yet to put on a pair of jeans, I have worn a purse only a handful of times, and I'm now super into sneakers—although I still wear my heels, obviously. My makeup skills have gotten pretty professional, too. I turned my bedroom into my at-home television studio, filming segments and Instagram Lives. I've gravitated toward a cat-eye, a bronze face, and glossy lips—a done-up look that still looks natural and effortless. As for my nails, my mom took on the role of manicurist for a while, first removing my gel manicure, which was nearly impossible. I don't even know how the professionals do it! If you have had that experience, you know.

The most surprising shift: I've become surprisingly proficient in DIY beauty treatments that I so heavily relied on others for in the past. I learned to do my own hair so well now I can't even imagine going back to getting blowouts! Of course, I miss getting spray tans with my go-to, Anna, but I've found amazing cream products that allow me to get a similar look at home (although I must admit my skin has gotten streaky at times and it took me a lot of mess-ups to find what works best for me).

STAY-AT-HOME TRENDS

Of course quarantine attire became all about comfort, but influencers still found ways to introduce new trends. Let's not forget the introduction of the hottest one of all: tie-dye. Not only was everyone buying tie-dye, they were making it! I was no exception, buying sweatshirts, sweatpants, t-shirts—even hair scrunchies! This became *the* pattern to wear and activity to do during self-isolation. Wearing tie-dye gave me a burst of positive energy, but actually making my own pieces was incredibly soothing and a great creative outlet. There was no way to screw it up; the messier, the better. A little '60s rebellion; everyone was wearing it and teaching others how to make it when scrolling through Instagram.

In addition to tie-dye's comeback, we were blessed with the newest quarantine accessory: face masks. This fashion accessory was for safety and protection, but of course designers found a way to make it trendy and glam. I knew it was getting out of control when I saw ads for bathing suits with coordinating masks.

I never thought that I'd ever see everyone I know covering their faces when leaving their homes—that is, those who actually decided to follow the mandate. But this wasn't really a choice. Without face coverings, we'd all be more exposed to this life-threatening virus.

What started off as an impossible find (N-95 masks), morphed into so much more: fashion designers all around the country started making masks in their style aesthetics, colors, and patterns. Now, months later, we buy face masks like it's totally normal. Interestingly face masks also became a way for designers who were suffering from COVID-19 related sales losses to survive. Especially designers in the eveningwear business, like Christian Siriano, pivoted seamlessly to mask manufacturing—and donating tons to hospitals; one thousand in just three days alone—since there were no longer nights out, big events, or red carpets. Many generous designers, like Michael Costello with his Million Mask Initiative, also donated masks to first line workers like nurses and food service workers. Influencers started using their platforms for charitable initiatives too. Former Real Housewife of New York, Jill Zarin, and her daughter, Ali, used their huge platform to launch "Noshes for Nurses" to feed hospital workers.

FROM THE WAIST UP

Instead of dressing up for nights out or IRL get-togethers, the new quest quickly became dressing for Zoom calls, a.k.a. the most popular app for communicating via video chat. From Zoom birthday parties to business meetings to first dates, Zoom quickly became the hub for all things communication, and it seems like it will remain a popular tool in years to come as many companies continue allowing their staff to work from home. The funny fashion part about Zoom calls is that most people look presentable on top, and in most cases wear comfy sweatpants or shorts on the bottom. I know for me, it will definitely be challenging to go back to wearing uncomfortable, more structured bottoms.

So, how do you dress for this new kind of get-together? These are my top ten tips to consider for any Zoom scenario you might encounter:

1. **Make a statement on top**: Remember, in a Zoom, only the top portion of your body will be shown, so this is where you want to make things most polished and stylish.

2. **Bring on the color**: Wearing a pop of color is a great way to stand out, whether you're in a meeting or on a date.

3. **Statement sleeves are a Go**: From a puffed shoulder to a cap sleeve, bring the attention right to your face!

4. **Refrain from Shiny Fabrics**: Cameras can easily pick up the shine of a blouse and provide some unflattering glare, especially if you wear a satin or transparent fabric.

5. **Looser Fits = More Flattering**: Most bodycon pieces look most flattering when standing, so when you're sitting—and depending on your lighting—a fitted outfit like a dress may not be the most flattering. If you want that sexier look then just wear a bodycon top.

6. **Accessorize:** Bring on the statement earrings or fashion-forward hair accessories to create a memorable look. Top-knot headbands from designer Lele Sadoughi or look-a-likes will definitely do the trick!

7. **Invest in a Ring Light**: A ring light is a circular, ring-shaped light on a tripod stand that photographers use to prevent shadows and create a flawless look. My ring light was downright my quarantine boyfriend. You can find different versions on Amazon. They cost anywhere from thirty to a hundred dollars or more, depending on the quality. The light facing you directly creates the most flattering of views and will clear up your image so everyone can see you and your outfit perfectly! You will be amazed at the difference in how you look versus other people and they will definitely comment about the flattering light. Make sure to adjust the brightness based on the natural light in the room. Also, this is a great time to add highlight to your makeup routine. You will simply glow with the ring light shining on you!

8. **Wear Makeup You're Comfortable With**: If you use a ring light, your face might look washed out, so this is the time to add a little bronzer, mascara, or a statement lip. No need for a full face if you don't want to, but a little makeup will definitely define your most flattering features! The overall quarantine trend was softer and more natural makeup. Going

forward, I think it is reasonable to go back to more of your normal palette.

9. **Think about dressing for the occasion**: If it's a first Zoom date, you probably want to be a bit sexy but not too provocative to get your date either too excited or scare him or her off. If it's a job interview, dress as you would if it were in person (and don't forget pants, trust me).

10. **Make an Impression**: It isn't truly face-to-face, but take time to think about the impression you want to create so that the person on the other end will look forward to an in-person meeting. I still think about my outfits for virtual meetings and dates as much as I would for one IRL. Value the importance and time equally, and don't treat them with anything less!

I've incorporated these tips into my quarantine and COVID-19-era lifestyle since the very beginning. Soon after the quarantine began in late-March, I launched a daily Instagram Live series called "Lunchtime with Sydney" to help people feel less alone during their remote lunch breaks. Through the series, I've had conversations with celebrities like Candace Cameron Bure and Rebecca Romijn, supermodel Maye Musk, fashion designers Michael Costello and Lele Sadoughi, celeb trainers Gunnar Peterson and Isaac Boots, legendary makeup artist Bobbi Brown, and so many others. So many of my guests, across industries, are people I've looked up to for many years. The series has over fifty thousand unique viewers—and counting. Through this experience, I've learned the best and worst outfits for video calls and have gotten creative in repurposing items in my closet.

Ultimately, times like these teach you how to pivot and allow you to reflect and realize what's important in life. I learned so much about myself throughout this time, but one thing that really has stuck with me is that how you dress can affect your mood and attitude. You wear the outfit; the outfit doesn't wear you. Clothing, even something as simple as rainbow tie-dye, can help you find control in your life, even when things feel so out of your hands. It's important during a global pandemic—and always—to love yourself even more than you thought you could. Some days, especially when you're stuck at home with no place to go, it can be easy to stay in sweats all day and feel hopeless. But if you learn how to *Aim High* and dress up even a little bit, it can help shift your mindset and change your perspective.

EPILOGUE:
BEHIND MY SCENES

I've always been a businesswoman.

—Kim Kardashian West

L ast Halloween, I was with an *Inside Edition* crew in the middle of Times Square during the after-work rush hour. We literally took over a full block! It was freezing cold, and, unfortunately, I was dressed in a light, silky, sexy black dress with high-heeled sandals. I was all set for the Halloween segment: commenting on costume trends, ranging from a sexy Mr. Rogers outfit, to a Felicity Huffman and Lori Loughlin jailbird ensemble and even a scary-looking Joaquin Phoenix *Joker* look.

Whether I'm in the television studio or on-location, "lights, camera, action!" is triggered—in the eyes of the public—when the red light on the camera facing me starts to blink.

But so often, people are shocked to learn that my work extends far beyond speaking on a show. In reality, the "action" phase starts much earlier than viewers realize, with an incredible amount of advanced planning, often for weeks at a time, leading up to each and every segment. Behind-the-scenes planning is key to the success of my segments. My role and responsibilities extend from concept creation and "selling" the idea to producing the televised segment and finally presenting a turnkey product.

Equally challenging, networks and national or local shows each offer different approaches to fashion segments and target demographics. The current trend focuses on attracting moms—the traditional female audience watching daytime television. Popular shows often feature live studio audiences; some are live in-studio with only the hosts and producers present; others are taped in-studio to air at a later date; while a number are taped on location. It all varies.

The behind-the-scenes work was no different for this *Inside Edition* piece. But to add even more stress to the live, on-location set-up was the unpredictable New York City fall weather.

Awaiting my turn on-camera, I ran in and out of the Sephora vestibule in Times Square in an attempt to warm up. There were no chairs in the store (only a skincare display), and attentive salespeople constantly approached us with well-intended (but alas distracting) offers of assistance. Little did they know that a warm escape from the cold was the biggest help we could have asked for.

Eventually, I found myself sitting on the side of a window, which seemed like a great option as opposed to the floor since standing for long hours was becoming painful, to say the least. Sure, I was getting frostbite, my mom frequented a nearby food kiosk for tea, minus the tea bag, so I could use the boiling water for my numb fingers and toes. I wrapped my sore fingers around the cup while she put my toes up against another cup. It was definitely one of those career moments when you go well above and beyond for your job, hoping there is a career rainbow at the end of the experience.

While filming, we were constantly bombarded by passersby trying to get in on the action. Curious onlookers tried to find out what we were filming and even tried to get on-camera. Distracting camera flashes from tourists hurt our eyes, and not long into the start of our shoot, the skies turned very dark. There were even a few uncomfortable moments with long stares and loitering around the costume models.

That segment is a perfect example of my reality: I don't know exactly how the segment will go until I arrive at the shoot. Will I be hosting it myself or commentating with a host interviewing me? The most important priority is to be totally prepared so that when the unexpected arises, I'm emotionally and physically available to conquer. This is a good rule of thumb for anything we do in life, too.

Adapt to whatever happens and maintain a positive attitude, which is easier said than done.

Critical for any job, a positive attitude can shape your reputation in the same way that a great outfit can. Achieving the best version of yourself and remaining professional at all times never goes out of style.

I've learned a lot of things through my life so far, and still do everyday, but one thing that I'm certain about is that life is full of ups and downs. One minute you think you're conquering the world and looking your best. Another minute, you feel totally opposite. And then it goes up again. And then maybe down a little. It's like a cycle, see what I mean? But that's what makes this life! It's constantly changing and evolving, and you mostly don't know what's going to happen next.

What I do know is this: if you put your mind to something, work super hard for it, and do everything that's possibly in your power to achieve the outcome you want, you will achieve your goals. I'm still on my journey, but I always think about the career rainbow that I mentioned earlier in this chapter. When you can taste it and see it in your dreams, that's when you know you're on the right path. Fashion has always been at the core and heart of what I do. It's what makes me confident, excited about life, and ultimately feel connected to the generations of people in my family who truly have shaped the woman I've become.

I hope you've learned throughout this book that fashion isn't just materialistic. Fashion is, at its core, something that can help you style your *life* and help you achieve everything you want. A little black dress can make you feel sexy and a pair of strappy shoes can change the way you walk into a room, but underneath, it's all you. Your personal style is something uniquely yours and *Aiming High* is about embracing who you are and going after your goals, even when they seem impossible. Don't you dare settle for anything less. You deserve it.

ACKNOWLEDGMENTS

The people below are key figures in my life and define what it means to Aim High.

I can't thank my mom, Amy, enough for everything she does for me, her unconditional support in who I am and what I do, and for being on my side in every way possible with all of my professional activities and throughout the process of this book. Whenever someone asks me who I look up to, it's hands down my mom. She is the definition of a true leader, a seasoned business professional who knows how to get things done and after decades of a successful career has transitioned to working with me. There isn't anyone who supports me or protects me more or frankly who I can trust. Mom—I love you infinitely.

Thank you to my brother Mitchell who is also such a force behind my thinking and ability to make my vision a reality. I could not have created the content that we made for announcing the book without him; particularly since we were in quarantine and were unable to work with an outside team. He is so talented and capable and can do anything he puts his mind to. I'm convinced he's the big brother and I'm the little sister, when in fact it is the other way around!

To my dad, who is as excited to promote what I do as much as I am, and always eager to share what I'm up to with his friends and colleagues. In the moments where it's hard to see the light, he always makes me laugh and see the positive side. Who else could I Face Time with multiple times a day just to "check in" with each other?!

I so wish my grandparents Marvin and Hannah, and my poppy Harry, who all passed within a short time of each other, were able to see and read this book. I would call my Grandpa Marvin multiple times a day to tell him everything I was working on and to ask for his advice. He was the one who first supported me leaving my desk job and going out to pursue my dreams. I know he wouldn't be surprised I accomplished writing this book. If anything, he would say, well of course you did it! Grandma Hannah was a huge inspiration for the content of this book. She was the first person to teach me about fashion and loved taking me shopping as a little girl. My Poppy, who was also just the most supportive person, was always there for me. He would get so proud every time I was on TV or published an article. Every time we talked on the phone, which was also daily, he'd tell me, "I pray for you every day to get everything you want out of your career." I know he'd be smiling. I miss all three of them so much.

My dear friend Francesco Bilotto—it's so funny because most of my closest friends have all been from elementary school or college, but not Francesco! We met later in life at an event for Busy Phillipps. We knew of each other professionally but hadn't met. Once we did, I feel like it was love at first sight! (Sorry, Pete!! Francesco's husband). In an industry that's so competitive I'm so grateful for his constant advice, support, lunches and regular phone calls!

And to my cousins Abby, Nicole, Alexander and Kyle. Abby knows the most about me next to my mom; a best friend but like a sister. Nicole who has the best style in our family and should really be a model. Alexander who keeps me up to date on what I should know in the business world. Finally, Kyle: the baby of the family but with the biggest ideas that make me even more motivated to have over the top goals.